YOU WILL
Hear My Voice

YOU WILL
Hear My Voice

A Collection of Inspirational Poems

RONNIE FLETCHER

ARPress

ILLUMINATING IDEAS,
EMPOWERING VOICES

ARPress
45 Dan Road Suite 5
Canton MA 02021
Hotline: 1(888) 821-0229
Fax: 1(508) 545-7580

Ordering Information:
Quantity sales. Special discounts are available on quantity purchases by corporations, associations, and others. For details, contact the publisher at the address above.

Printed in the United States of America.

ISBN-13:	Softcover	979-8-89356-489-1
	eBook	979-8-89356-488-4

Library of Congress Control Number: 2024902677

My Road to Poetry

By Ronald Fletcher

It all started in April 2010 one afternoon when I received a call from my brother, Vincent Fletcher, one of my six brothers. Vincent was seen for many years because of his interactions in the drug game. He lived a "fast and furious lifestyle" and made it his business to have no association with my family. So it was surprising to me when my phone rang one day and it was Vincent on the other end! Vincent stated, *"Ronnie I need you to come and see me. I'm in the hospital and I've been told that I have cancer! I need you to do me a favor.* "Startled by his statement I responded, "Hold Up! I haven't seen or heard from you in years! Now you call me for a favor! That's not right, but I will come anyway."

The next day I went to visit my brother. When I arrived he had tears in his eyes. He thanked me for coming and began to speak. "I need a favor from you".

I responded, "Wait a minute! You really only called me for a favor?"

He then stated," Please do this favor for me." I pulled up a chair next to his bedside and sat down to listen. He then began to cry as he stated," Ronnie, I know it was wrong for me to live the way I did, but I changed! I don't sell drugs anymore. I go to church every Sunday and have found The Lord! The favor that I ask of you is to go to church with me and sit in my seat to represent me until I get out of the hospital." His eyes then filled with tears as he began to then state," My lady will go with you to show you where I sit."

That was the moment I took his hand and asked for the name of the church. Vincent sat up in his bed and said, "Bethel Gospel Assembly in Harlem located on 120thStreet and Madison Avenue." He then said, "Can you do this favor for me until I get released from the hospital?" I then looked at my younger brother and said," Church?!? That's the favor you ask of me; to go to church! We have five other brothers that you could have asked! Why would you choose me out of all of us? What else would you like from me? That's when I repeated one again... Church?!? Vincent, do you know that I done do church, so why ask ME for this?"

He stated, "God told me to ask you!"

I shouted, "Excuse me! Did you say God told you?" I smiled and said," Oh really! What else did God tell you Vincent?" Vincent looked at me with a straight face and stated," That's it!" He then said, "Please Ronnie I need you to do this for me!"

I than began to look up at the sky and state,"Ok Vincent. I will go and fill your seat this Sunday. Tell your lady to meet me at the church tomorrow." Vincent thanked me and told me that the service started at 11am.

The next day I went to the church that my brother mentioned and was confronted by five gentlemen standing in front of the church. One of the men was a man who I later found out was called Deacon Stretch. He stopped me and introduced himself as a friend of my brother Vincent. He asked me could he have a moment of my time in order to pray for my brother Vincent before we entered the church. My suspicions led me to believe something was going on at this place. The man reached for my hand and led me to a circle where they began praying for my brother Vincent. While they were praying, my eyes filled up with tears and I started getting goose bumps throughout my body; but I still remained silent. Once they finished their prayer we headed inside. That's when I asked, "How do you know who I am?" My brother's girlfriend came over and said," Hello Ronnie. My name is Neraida. I'm Vincent's girlfriend. We met at the hospital. Remember me? Vincent told me to inform you them that you were coming today."

Once the introductions were completed, I followed them to the seat my brother normally filled. The service began and all I could do was observe all the friendly people around me. During the service a lady came to the podium to speak. The lady introduced herself and said, "I am a profit and I believe the Holy Spirit is here today."

She then stated, "Today some of you are going to feel the Spirit today. I want every one of you who aren't working to stand up and I want every one of you who are working to touch those people so that they may feel

God's touch!" That's when my brother's girlfriend told me to reach out to the lady next to me and touch her. I than began to reach out and touch her shoulder. She began to tremble! I then took my hand off of her in a state of shock! Vincent's girlfriend then said, "No Ronnie don't take your hand off, put it back on her again!" With great hesitation, I placed my hand on her a second time. Shen then began to tremble again. Startled by her reaction, I pulled my hand away a second time. Then I told Vincent's girlfriend, "I'm not touching her again, so don't ask!"

Nothing else happened that day. That night I went home to rest up because I had to work the next morning. During the night, I awake at 4am. This was strange to me because rarely have I ever awakened throughout the night. There were no sounds, no radio, no television, nothing but a voice telling me to write e a poem…. I sat up in my bed startled. I began to look around the dark room when I heard the voice say once again to write a poem! I then shouted who is this and what poem? I had never written a poem in my life. The voice said it a third time but this time it was a more commanding and stronger voice shouting "WRITE THE POEM!!!!" that's when I responded back "I have to go to work tomorrow!" I was dazed and confused and was baffled by the voice I was hearing. I tried to go back to sleep and brush it off but I began to toss and turn. After ten minutes of restlessness I got up from my bed and went into my dining room. I collected a pen and paper and sat down without lights. I then said, "I don't know who you are, but YOU WRITE THE POEM!!! I need to go to work tomorrow!"

My hand began to write effortlessly that night. I couldn't even see my words. My thoughts just attached themselves to my pen as my pen etched the symbols to paper!

The poem was called, "THANK YOU!!!"

Once I completed the poem, I was able to go to sleep. The next day went back to visit my brother in the hospital. When I arrived my brother's girlfriend was sitting there. As I entered the hospital room, my brother smiled and asked about my visit to the church. Before I could answer his question, I began to tell him about my experience from last night. My brother smile as he sat in the bed. He began to say, "Ronnie, the Lord visited you last night and now you are anointed! The Lord has blessed you Ronnie. You must pray to The Lord. The Lord will find favor for you. Please pray!"

I stated, "Vincent, I don't know how to pray. Remember I don't go to church."

My brother sat up in the bed and began to pray. While he prayed, I just watched him. That's when Vincent's girlfriend stated, "Put your hand on your brother."

I turned to her and said, "OH no! You're not starting this crap again. Are you?"

She stated. "Please touch your brother while he is praying for you." I decided to humor her and place my hand on my brother's shoulder. When I touched my brother his words changed from words I could understand to words that I could not. The language he began to speak and the voice I heard wasn't his anymore. My brother scared me and when I commenced to take my hand off his shoulder, I couldn't! I felt something pressing my hand in place and locking it in that position. My brother continued to pray and that same voice and language that I hadn't heard before. Even as I tried to move away from my brother, I couldn't. After five minutes, my brother stopped speaking and my hand was released. I then stumbled away from the side of his hospital bed. My brother's doctor then entered the room and asked if I was a family member. I then stated, "Yes!" The doctor then turned to my brother and stated that he had some bad news to share. He began to explain to him that his cancer had increased to stage four. He explained that there was nothing that could be done to help my brother except to transfer him to Calvary Hospital to give him comfort throughout the last stages of his illness. He stated that my brother only had two weeks to live!

The doctor then walked out of the room showing no empathy or sympathy for my brother's situation. He was cold as ice! My brother then began to cry. I then asked him what is wrong with him. My brother yelled, "What do you mean? Didn't you just hear what the doctor said? How can you be so insensitive?"

That's when I said," Listen to me. After all I've seen and have been through you're worried about that quack! Let me tell you something! God's not ready for you. This is why he told you to call me. I will be here for you. I will continue to visit you until you get better. I will follow you to the next hospital and see you walk out of there. You will recover from this. You will smile and enjoy life as you know it. You will enjoy family and friends again and will have more than the two weeks the doctor told you! The most important thing is that you walk out of this hospital and you and I revisit the church together because I am not going there alone every Sunday!"

My brother transferred to Calvary Hospital and recovered and was escorted out of the hospital. We both went to church the Sunday following his return home. As I sat with my brother in church that Sunday after his homecoming, I decided to become a church member. I was then introduced by my brother to the Bishop of the church and many of my brother's church friends. We started a ritual of going to church together every Sunday. My brother was also able to go back to work and was also able to begin spending time with family.

Two years later, my brother became ill yet again. His cancer had returned and he was once again admitted to the hospital. His girlfriend called me to come to his bedside. One night as I was alone with my brother in his hospital room I took his hand and thanked him. I told him, "Vincent, your job was to bring me out of the wilderness into Church. The Lord has called me to continue your walk. He is now waiting for you with open arms."

My brother's eyes filled with tears as he began to transition to be with The Lord. As he was dying I began to realize that all the poems I wrote are spiritual memories, testimonies about people walking out on faith and the experiences they share. Because of the Holy Spirit, I have ten books published and two more to complete. I hope the world reads the words that I have written because God is real and I have a story to tell.

My journey has just begun! I know my brother is listening as I say to him,

"JOB WELL DONE!"

—Ronald Fletcher (2019)

Contents

You Will Hear Me.. 1

A Child's Voice 2

Do You See Me? 3

The Undercover Boss 4

Daddy, Why? 5

The Real You 6

Your Choice 7

What's Your Memory? 8

Can You Accept Me? 9

Why Should I Help Another? 10

Your Mission 11

Daddy Issues 12

The Fight Within You.. 13

Walk With Me 14

Grieve 15

Someone Must Die.. 16

I Find You Guilty...17

Do You Understand? 18

Help Me Daddy 19

The Plan 20

Hold On 21

Confess 22

Where Would I Be? 23

Expectations.. 24

Lost In The Past.. 25

The Push... 26

My Friend 27

I Got Some Bad News... 28

You Didn't Appreciate Me 29

Tears 30

What Must I Do 31

Great Expectations 32
Stop Asking The Lord Why 33
Dig A Little Deeper 34
Our Father is Upset 35
Do You Really Understand? 36
A Father's Pain 37
You Need to Learn 38
The Lord's Eye Test 39
Thank You For 40
My Gratitude Letter 41
Your Yesterday 42
Your Mask 43
Fellas 44
Grace Of Today 45
The Tears On My Face 46
Finding You 47
Hello You 48
The Interview 49
Are You Ready To Fight 50
Good Morning Pain 51
Do You Remember Me 52
Where Are You At? 53
My Today 54
The Lord Asked Where Are You At? 55
I Called Out To You 56
You're Never Alone 57
I'm Ready To Fight 58
The Real Family 59
I Can't Cry For You 60
Selfish 62
A Wedding Vow 63
I Didn't Know 64
The Hand Of Thee 65
Hello My Heart 66
The Lost And Found Of A Man 67
What's Your Memory? 68

Pride Vs Trust 69

Why Should I Help Another 70

Let's Make Things Right! 71

Mama Please! 72

Couldn't Sleep Last Night! 73

It Wasn't Me 74

The Trial 75

Suffer No More 76

Why Have You Forgotten Me? 77

A New Day! 78

A Lonely Night 79

A Pain From The Past 80

He Felt The Lord's Touch 81

You Will All Be Tested 82

I Gave You 83

What You Didn't Do! 84

Hate Won't Win... 85

A Daughter Will Always Want Her Daddy 86

Who Are You? 87

Let Me 88

Don't Complain 89

How Many Times Did You? 90

Mommy How I Miss You... 91

You Have Issues... 92

I'm Proud Of You.. 93

Why Are We? 94

Not Me 95

When You Lose It All... 96

The Loss Of A Loved One 97

The Devil Asked For You... 98

She Said "I Love You Daddy".. 99

Today Is A Good Day 100

Hello Tomorrow!..101

I Remember You 102

Daddy Please..103

Couldn't Sleep Last Night 104

Let's Make Things Right... 105
A New Day 106
Sit Down And Listen 107
The Monster From Within.. 108
We Need To Cry.. 109
That's My Child..110
Where I've Been 111
Are You Ready To Confess?...112
I Feel You..113
What's The Plan 114
Are You Ready For The Rain? 115

The reason there's only 114 poems in each of
my books is because of my brother Vincent Fletcher.
His birthday was 04/11 and he passed away on 10/14.

These two dates combines into 114.

These books are in memory of him.

You Will Hear Me

Each day you wake up is another day of My grace
I want you to think about what you've earned in your space
While you may want something new every single day
The time has come for you to hear what your Lord has to say
How did you become what you are if not by the hand of Thee
When did you become bigger than the world created by Me
While you live and breathe I want you to fully understand
You live for My plan and that is the divine
purpose of every woman and man
Behold My message, because one day I will return to the earth
Just know your day will come when you will
understand and appreciate My worth
When I speak you will become humbled by My voice
You will be startled, afraid, and show the fear I
bring when you won't have a choice
Who ever told you that you will be bigger than THEE
Learn to know My word because I will make sure you will hear Me
The time will come when I will reach down for your soul
As I watch your actions on earth to see if you did as you were told
The time will arrive when I will tell you your time has come
As your soul will tremble with fear before
you return to where you're from
While you enjoyed My grace, you seem to ignore the call of Thee
Get ready for My call because I will make sure you HEAR ME!

A Child's Voice

Last night while I was asleep there was a voice
Crying so loud that it woke me up…I had no choice
With tears on my face I jumped out of my bed
Not knowing who was crying as my face became so red
My tears were so large that they blinded my eyes
Yet all I could do is sit up and look to the skies
What I realized was that the cries came from a child
Yet there wasn't any child around but I still couldn't smile
The cries that I heard were for help of a child's pain
The tears that I felt were covered by the rain
Help me Lord because I'm drowning in this troubled world
While the cries became so loud from every boy and girl
Help me father to understand my troubled way
That was the moment that the child heard its Father say
Come to Me my children and listen to My word
Read the Bible I have given and remember the voice you heard
I will always be with you as you walk in My wilderness
You will have moments of trouble but make sure to remember this
Each step you take through life will be one I take with you
Just trust that your Father will always watch what you do
Never feel abandoned, just remember you will always have a choice
Trust in My spirit within you, and allow your steps to follow My voice

Do You See Me?

Now this is a question that is so often asked by Thee
While we live each day the Lord ask do you see Me
You may not know the Lord as a woman or a man
But when He is a part of your daily life you begin to understand
Each day that you awaken from your quite night of sleep
This was another night that you were protected by the Lord's keep
The Lord works every day, even while we rest
Meeting every challenge as He shelters our rest
While we wonder if the Lord is with us at every turn
How long will it take before His presence is acknowledged as we learn
When the Lord gives a blessing and His presence is felt
Knowing that the Lord is with us, allows us to confront what is dealt
How long before we acknowledge the troubles that we fear
The answer is in the Word that non-believers refuse to hear
How long before we stand up and tell the devil we are ready to fight
Come to the battle ground prepared to say "you won't win tonight"
The Lord is always present even when you ask "how could this be?"
Instead of feeling down, look up while the Lord asks" Do you see me?"

The Undercover Boss

Tonight I saw a show that brought me to tears
While owners search the world to erase employee's fears
While we meet strangers in our lives every single day
Never did I see anyone change a stranger's life this way
Each day that we live is another moment that we cross
While we live each moment never expecting an undercover boss
Everybody has a dream that one day they will receive a gift
Hoping for a miracle or maybe a spiritual lift
Lord we call on You because it's your world that we embrace
While we go through our own struggles with tears upon our face
Yet once in a while a blessing comes in an unusual way
Hopeful to receive and appreciate the blessing of today
Lord I come before You with open arms on my knees
Humbled with tears of joy feeling the Holy Spirit's breeze
As you lift all my burdens and show the world Your force
I've been blessed by the touch of the world's Undercover Boss

Daddy, Why?

Today there are so many men who want to cry
When they think of their past it asks the question why
The questions their children have may never be revealed
Yet the answers that are requested could change the whole deal
Daddy why did you forget all about your daughter or your son
The fathers of yesterday seemed to be around only for some fun
Daddy while you were younger and decided to pick up my mother
What were your intentions; because you could have chosen another
Daddy even when you decided that I was yours to care for
Why did you decide to leave out of the front door
Now Daddy there were times when you came home late at night
Just because we lived under the same roof
didn't make your actions alright
Daddy your children felt that you really didn't seem to care
Why did you leave all the responsibilities and Mommy with her tears
So many men of today have daddy issues because he wasn't around
So many excuses, blame and abuse that made every child frown
This is the reason why the men of today are so confused by their roles
Just think of all the absent men who were never there for their role
The reason why so many men are so angry without any reason
They are victims of their childhood because
their own father committed treason
So ladies check your man's past and understand why he cries
Allow them to reveal their past as they ask their own DADDY, WHY

The Real You

Last night I thought about what we do
While I sat down thinking about the real you
Each day that we shared wasn't what you advertised
Sold me a lot of hope and dreams that never seemed to materialized
While we lived in the moment that was so wonderful
Each time you left me alone I became so grateful
Thinking about the next time we would have together
Only to be disappointed because of our stormy weather
Not everything promised can be given at any moment in time
Yet each moment that I cherished seem to end like a crime
Why did you make me believe that you were the one
While I hungered for your love only to find you to be on the run
Your beauty caught my attention as you moved in for the kill
The warm kiss of your lips gave my body the ultimate kind of thrill
Hunger for more of you wasn't any kind of surprise
Thinking of a future became so clear to my starving eyes
Your words, your touch, your emotions caught the best of me
Yet now I've become a victim of the real you
who yells out saying let me be
Why have you captured my heart only to break it in two
Now I'm broken from the pain that has found the real you

Your Choice

Come together everyone because your time has come
While you enjoy or cry for all to learn to be grateful under my sun
Each person you meet occupies a chair at My table
Everyone does what they believe they can while they are able
While we pass through life it's only for a given moment
Nobody understands why they were even sent
Each chair in life has a table which holds a memory
Don't ever forget your place at the table which is set by Thee
When you sit at the table and allow to be blessed with food
Don't ever forget to be grateful because that would be so rude
Before you dig in to enjoy the meal set before you
You have been given a chair for the Lord's own reason
Learn to appreciate the fact that this grace may only last for a season
There are so many people who may never fill the Lord's chair today
So understand the blessing that was made in GOD'S way
Not everyone shares a table with their own sister or a brother
Not everyone ever gets to sit down with their
real father or their real mother
So the next time you sit down with a friend or any family
Before you say grace, just look at your
surroundings and be grateful to THEE
Life has many changes and we all have a moment that doesn't seem fair
Just be grateful for the table as you have been
blessed to fill another one of God's chairs

What's Your Memory?

We all have moments that we wish we could remember
Whether it's today or yesterday; either June or September
While our memory is all that we have to live for
How could we ever live in the moment yet ask for even more
This time or next time are all turned to a memory
Yet we continue to live on asking how this could be
Through hard times and easy moments we try to live right
While we wonder how could our happy days turn into scary nights
When you think back to a moment some will bring a smile
So which of your moments brings you to act like a child
Not every moment brings you to a happy moment in your past
Can you think back to when you felt that our happiness couldn't last
Cherish each day and be grateful when they are great
Take a moment you regret as you're granted a clean slate
Not everyone will be able to say thank you for getting a new way
Did you ever think you would be given a chance for a new today
Rise up from your day because we aren't promised another
Help all who you can, whether they are your sister or your brother
The Lord has delivered you from the devil's
hands and allowed you to see
Live in the moment and remember the blessed times of your memory

Can You Accept Me?

The Lord came to me last night with a simple question
Startled by His voice He made one simple suggestion
Instead of being like everyone that you're used to
I've come to you in spirit so I could talk with you
Now pull up a chair because I have a lot to say
The world you live in is not what I intended
Yet so many have sinned and for this I feel very offended
The world is in a place that needs Me to take a stand
So I have come to reveal My anger on every woman and every man
Because very few will listen to what I have to say
The time is coming for Me to end this world My way
My anger will be revealed and the end will come soon
There is no way to tell the sinners of the night or afternoon
You, My son have listened without judgement of Thee
So I will reveal the future of the world and you will remain with Me
Too many times I have forgiven this world only to hear more lies
Yes; I hear the pain of everyone, and yes I also hear their cries
Yet as I look past their words I also search their hearts
The actions that are revealed shows Me denial from the very start
So My son, spread My word and tell all you
know the message from Thee
The Lord told me to ask everyone "can you accept Me?"

Why Should I Help Another?

Today I walked down a street and was approached by a man
All the people walking by this stranger and yet I could fully understand
Each step that I had taken was a moment set up by Thee
How the Lord gave me another one of His own opportunities
While I walked down this street observing several strangers in need
What if the role was reversed I thought,
needing help of my mouth to feed
When you take the time to think about what life could be
That should be the moment you should be
grateful of your own life from Thee
So many people would change places with what the Lord has given you
Just to have what you throw away and we all know that this is true
There are so many organizations that provide help or some type of relief
Yet because our coldness has gotten to a point
that we have become the real thief
Look around you and see how people suffer in every type of way
Please tell me how you would feel if all of a
sudden life treated you this way
When you see a stranger asking for food and a little change or anything
Just take a moment to consider what a little kindness could surely bring
Hopefully one day you will realize that what has
been given can surely be taken away
Those homeless, less fortunate people you
meet didn't always live this way
When you turn away and judge someone because of how they look
Think about who you are and when you didn't
have and tell me "who's the crook?"
Your mission in life if you decide to accept,
should be to help who you can
Learn to accept your blessings as you begin to truly understand
When you see that stranger on the street who
could be your sister or brother
That will be your answer as to why you should help another

Your Mission

Attention everyone because I will need your permission
To examine your past or to shed a light on your mission
First let's exam what you're really all about
Let's think about the real you who just loves to scream and shout
Then we should address those who feel they have been saved
The time has come to explain why you don't know how to behave
Do you really think about others the same as you do yourself
Have you taken the time to share or did you
place that thought on a shelf
Do you extend your heart to a stranger who had a need
Have you ever thought that not helping is
a sign of your own selfish greed
While you ponder these questions, I have so many more
Yet this might get too heavy a topic and have you rushing out the door
What if I told you that you exist only to help a stranger
What if I showed you that without helping
another, you could be in danger
What if I told you the time will come when you must give
The real question is, are you ready for that moment
when you will change how you live
When the Lord taps you on your shoulder it
will be to get your full attention
You will feel your whole body get a chill and this
will be a moment you'll want to mention
When the Lord touches you and He will, He
doesn't wait for your permission
That will be your divine moment as He
reveals your own personal mission

Daddy Issues

Good morning everyone! I think it's time to set the record straight
While we live and breathe, we have our own
issues that determine our own fate
Each person in this world has a daddy that
they want to get to really know
Some have their real dad around while others question why he had to go
We are all a product of how we had to grow up and live
Some of us have regrets while others are taught how to forgive
There are so many children who grew up without their own daddy
While their mothers tried to maintain a
childhood and support the family
Most boys grew up in a household that they couldn't understand
Because they were the only person in the
house who could be called the man
Most girls need their father to keep them in his eye
Yet so many girls lose their father and will
never know the real reason why
While boys grow up and feel one day they will become a man
Yet without daddy around, how could they ever really understand
A boy needs his father to show him the right way
Yet if their father wasn't around, how could
he ever show his son his yesterday
Some children grow up hating the daddy that they never even knew
Until their father's truth arrives and they cry out "Daddy I miss you!"
So if your father is around, just forgive whatever he did to you
Because everybody needs help when it comes to their own daddy issues

The Fight Within You

Last night while everyone was fast asleep
I laid in my bed so restless because my soul wouldn't keep
Each time tossing and turning only to stay awake
It was your spirit that I asked the Lord to take
So I got up from my bed and started to think
Only to feel your Holy Spirit filling me to the brink
I asked your spirit what was wrong, what could I do
That's when your spirit told me that it needed my rescue
The spirit that's known isn't the one that you show
While I travel with a smile only to hide
within the one that no one knows
Depressed and upset because I have to hide the real me
What will it take for the devil to set my real spirit free
When I heard your spirit reveal the torment that it held inside
Tears came to my eyes that I could no longer hide
Your Holy Spirit called on the Lord and asked Him what I needed to do
That was when the Lord answered I will rescue you
My son, I am here for all who want to begin
Surrender yourself to Me so your soul can feel it's win
I forgive all who want to enter into My holy Kingdom
No matter what path you have lived because I know where you're from
Surrender yourself to Me and I will forgive all that you've done
Just know who I am as you surrender to the Holy One
You have been given the path of what you must do
Prepare yourself for the victory as the Lord battles the fight within you

Walk With Me

Good morning everyone who had to face a moment of fear
Those who have received some troubling
news that they didn't need to hear
While you woke up this morning with tears on your face
Whoever would have imagined the saddest
news would be delivered with grace
When you received that phone call with the heart wrenching news
Scared by the ringing that would not allow your spirit to refuse
While you laid in your bed and allowed the phone to ring
Knowing for someone to call this late would only mean a sad thing
As you answered the phone and listened with great hesitation
Only to be informed of the bad news of this alarming information
Yet you braced yourself at the moment to receive this call
Leaving your heart so devastated that you couldn't move at all
That's the moment when your body feels such a drain
Because the sad news you just received leaves your heart in great pain
The time has come for you to rise up on to your feet
Yet are you ready for the darkness that you are about to meet
A loved one, a family member or maybe a close friend
Who has been called by the Lord to be shown their blessed end
People don't realize that when you're called on by Thee
This is a blessing when the Lord says "come walk with Me"

Grieve

A dramatic situation has just happened in your life
The loss of a loved one has stabbed you like a knife
Sad for the moment without any type of warning
While the storm of this pain leaves us very puzzled this morning
What happened to our loved one who brought so many memories
As we sit in shock of the loss of someone too close to me
Where do I go so that the pain will go away
Never can a person prepare for this type of pain we feel today
While family and friends may come by to help you grieve
Nobody can truly understand what you refuse to receive
As people gather to pay their own type of respect
Most who come to visit this moment are only here to reflect
How many will remember moments shared; most won't have a clue
While we mourned and cried out about how they affected you
This will be a day that you can try to hold back your tears
Yet as you go down your own memory lane
to reflect on those happy years
Not everyone will share your own point of view
So hold on to the memory that the loved one gave to you
Today your loved one needs your memory to be believed
This will be your time to reflect as you begin to Grieve

Someone Must Die

Today was a special day because it was a strong lesson
While the pastor spoke of the cross which revealed a confession
As we sat down in the church on this new Palm Sunday
Everyone came to hear the message given in a holy way
The pastor cleared his throat and put a smile on his face
While everyone gave their attention as the Holy Spirit filled God's place
The Pastor made a statement that made everyone question why
While we all listened closely as the Pastor stated someone must die
Let me explain my statement; in order for you to live someone must die
The pastor paused for a moment to allow the babies to cry
The world is a cycle and please let me explain
Look at the food you eat, doesn't it come at
the expense of an animal's pain
Animals are killed so that you can eat food everyday
If the animals weren't killed, if the plants weren't
gathered, we wouldn't have another day
How could we ever eat the food given from the sky
Jesus knew of the cycle and He understood why He had to die
While His followers cried their tears when
Jesus was displayed on the cross
He asked His father to forgive the actions of all of us
Even to this day we will always ask the question why
Yet we now understand the cycle; to live, someone must die

I Find You Guilty

Good morning Your Honor as I stand before THEE
Without ever having a trial the Lord asked "are you guilty?"
Before I could answer, the Lord asked "do you know why you are here?"
Puzzled by the question as my soul revealed my fear
Let Me begin with the charges brought against you
While I review your life and the events of what you won't do
As I turned to find a chair so that I could sit down
The Lord asked me "do you think I'm fooling around?"
With a strong voice I heard Him say STAND UP AND FACE ME!
Don't ever judge or question Me or I will find you guilty
Fear came to me when I heard His strong voice
Listen and learn from this experience because you do have a choice
That was the moment that the Lord stated "lets
read the charges against you now"
As another voice reviewed my life story all I could say was WOW
Do you remember all the times the Lord's voice called on you
Do you remember your moments when you
responded I have something else to do
Do you remember when you were told to go help another
Do you remember your response by saying "I'm not their mother"
Do you remember when you questioned "who do you think you are?"
Do you remember when the Lord informed you that you've gone too far
Finally the voice ended after reading all the negative things in my life
Feeling so sad as if the voice had stabbed me in the gut with a knife
That was the moment when the voice said
"remain standing and face THEE"
By the power invested by the Holy Spirit "I FIND YOU GUILTY"

Do You Understand?

Today I heard a preacher who spoke a very powerful word
While he addressed the congregation, it was his message that I heard
When you meet a stranger and reach out to shake their hand
Have they already judged you by your appearance
without understanding the man
While we all use our vision to accept or begin to deny
The Bible teaches us not to judge others yet we all ask the question why
When you think about the term "you really don't understand me"
Does anyone take the time to understand or do they just let you be
We are all created in the image of the Holy One
Yet we live out each moment not ever doing what needs to be done
Have you ever taken the time to get to understand who you are
If not, then how can you judge someone else if
you've never thought of life thus far
Each time you awake is another day for you to understand
Yet when the sun sets, are you any closer to understanding God's plan
Have you ever tried to understanding yourself or why you even exist
Tell me are you afraid of the answer that might
be revealed when you reminisce
How can anyone say they love you without
ever understanding the real you
Have they fallen for their own eye's view, their
own lust, do they even have a clue
How many times have you told someone that
you don't understand the real me
When they begin to pay attention to the signs,
they question how this could be
When they grow to love and understand you, the real you is revealed
Will they still be there for you or have they requested a whole new deal
So today we ask the question for everybody who ever asked Thee
What will you do for my love, friendship, honesty,
commitment if you don't understand me

Help Me Daddy

I woke up this morning with a very heavy heart
While I had to recall her life yet not knowing where to start
When you think about your children it takes you to another place
As time passes by about the memories that can bring tears to your face
When you have several children you must keep their memories apart
Because every child has their own path which makes your thought start
Each child will have a moment when they will call out for you
The real question is will you be ready an understand what to do
Now many people who have children and
don't think about their yesterday
Will be reminded of the fact that life always
comes back in some type of way
You cannot prepare for the when or where your child will call out
Are you ready for their storm when they need to scream and shout
Your emotions will come show the mask that you usually wear
So how will you handle the call when it's your child that you hear
Are you there when your child needs to feel your own hand
When you're not around can you handle if they
seek someone else to understand
What effort have you ever made to become a part of their life
Have you become the solution or the problem
that had them seek the devil's knife
Every child needs a parent because this will guide them to succeed
Where are you when they call for guidance that they will need
When the parent fails to answer the call from their own child
Only God is the answer for their call; even if it takes awhile
Please understand the job of a parent is to teach their child about THEE
When you fail, just know He's the only help when
they call the words "help me DADDY"

The Plan

Today I heard a story that brought me to tears
While I had a lot of food, I never realized all my fears
While so many people go hungry each day for food and water
Yet I never thought about how blessed are my own sons and daughters
Each day there are so many people who live without
Some never have these problems and can't understand what that's about
Each night that I'm able to go home to a nice house
Should be my sole reason that I should be quite as a mouse
Do we take a moment to realize where we could be
Troubled, homeless, handicapped for life as we cry out to THEE
Each person has a problem that they consider such a task
Yet there are people with much less and they refuse to ask
When you see a homeless person living out on the streets
Asking for your help of any kind to get them on their feet
When you see a child who you know made some bad choices
Can you become their blessing with good
advice and become their new voices
Heroes are made every day, yet we don't know who they are
Because they become someone's blessing without ever going too far
So the next time someone ask you can you give me a hand
Grant that stranger's request because you will become God's plan

Hold On

There will be times when we feel like it's the end
While there's no one to call on to just be a friend
There will be hard times and we will need to just stand down
As we look for a solution and there isn't one to be found
The time will come when you seek another person's advice
Yet when a loved one calls out will you ever need to think twice
When you love someone and they turn to you for a helping hand
Will you be able to be their friend and completely understand
Have you ever felt you were someplace you didn't belong
Yet when your name was called, were you able to say hold on
Not everyone is worthy of your help in their time of need
Could you be strong enough to forgive their moment of greed
Nobody is perfect and yet we all need to find forgiveness
Are you strong enough to tell an enemy that
you can help them through this
Reach out to a stranger and tell them I'm here for you
Ask them what's wrong and what are you able to do
Not everyone you meet will make you feel like you belong
The time will come for understanding as you yell out hold on
The time has come for everyone to rise up and come together
How else will we be able to confront this stormy weather
When all else fails and you hear the music of a favorite son
Find a stranger in need of a hug while you whisper to them to hold on

Confess

So many people in this world claim to do their best
Yet the Lord knows better and needs everyone to confess
Each morning you rise from the comfort of a bed
Not everyone has this luxury because they may have been misled
While some people feel they are entitled to live and breathe
This is a misunderstanding that shows the devil can deceive
Take a moment out of your busy day and look back at your path
Did you really believe that without the Lord
you could survive the devil's wrath
Yet all I ask of you is to acknowledge My love for you
This is a simple thing that you still refuse to do
Each bump in your road causes you to remember to call out My name
Why should I help someone like you who only seeks Me to blame
How long will you hide from the love that I've shown you
Standing in harm's way, taking the hurt that comes from what you do
Tell me why you continue to avoid the simple task at hand
Your Father in heaven asked a question to every woman and man
You continue to cry out and question why these things happen to you
Stand up and acknowledge that you have become the devil's new toy
Don't come to Me until you're ready for My ultimate test
Kneel before your Father, surrender to Me as you begin to confess

Where Would I Be?

Today I had to pull up a chair and sit down
While things seamed okay, I needed to stop fooling around
Today I had to take a moment to look at me
While the reflection I saw asked how I could let this be
Each time I had to think of what I've been through
The next question I would ask was why God chose you
So while I thought about my personal journey
It was then that I began to realize how I've been guided by Thee
Where would I be if it wasn't for the Lord's hand
What and why? I would question the moments I couldn't understand
Where would I be if it wasn't for the Lord stepping in
The results would be dramatic and I really couldn't even begin
Where would I be if it wasn't for the path of the Lord
These thoughts, scary, yet they were ideas I couldn't afford
Where would I be if the Lord didn't place His angels in my path
This is a thought that's too scary to think
of before I feel the Lord's wrath
Where would I be if He allowed me to go through life on my own
The results are so scary to think I would be left all alone
So the next time you think you've been abandoned by Thee
Ask yourself the real question, "where would I be?"

Expectations

Good morning, didn't you expect to wake up today
Did you ever think about how you became so entitled in your own way
Life has a way of giving you things that you haven't earned
So my question is what have you truly learned
While we expect to live and breathe without even a fight
Didn't you expect life to go on every day and night
Let's take a moment and ponder the events of yesterday
As you review what happened to you without once kneeling to pray
Each day you take a chance before you step into the devil's fire
Yet there comes a time when you call out that the devil's a liar
How can things happen to you or for you when you don't get involved
What did you expect the Lord to do, just simply say they're solved
Miracles can only happen to you if you allow them through you
So are you still expecting change to arrive
without you doing what you need to do
Things happen every day to people that they can't begin to explain
Some lose their mind at what happens while others simply go insane
Yet they haven't really lost anything, they just accept their change
When the Lord delivers another miracle
some are grateful at the exchange
Most of all you will need to begin your own GOD relation
That will be the moment you realize your Lord has His own expectations

Lost In The Past

Take a moment to think of where you've been
Did you ever think hard times would allow you to win
Each time that you tried to move forward you always became derailed
Why did your course lead you to the point you felt you failed
How could you ever find the real person you're meant to be
When each time you cancelled the next step
toward your own opportunity
Why do you continue to look behind your steps of where you've been
Only to fall behind in a game that you surely can't win
The past is a place that you are supposed to learn from
How can you move forward if you can't handle what you've done
While you always say that you are now ready to move on
Yet the actions that you show seem to play the same old song
Who are you kidding when you claim your past is the past
When the question of healing comes up, your answer is not so fast
Pain comes from learning and understanding what you've been through
The question you need to answer is what are you willing to do
How can you find your way out of the woods without trying
While you wander blindly only to realize you've been lying
One day you will take the steps to test what's in the world
Pain and happiness is a result experienced by every boy and girl
So take off the blinders because life will be coming at you so fast
Learn to enjoy your journey before you become lost in the past

The Push

Today I heard the word from an anointed young man
While I was a little reluctant to ever begin to understand
As the bishop introduced this young man to the stage
My disbelief of his anointment was released from my own cage
The man started his message by speaking of David the king
While I adjusted my position to hear the message he would bring
So many people complain about their bumps on their road
The question is do they ever take a minute to
witness what the Lord has to unload
So many people live their life wishing for better days
When will they ever acknowledge their own effort toward a better way
The Lord gave us all a script that was written in His own word
Why do we choose to ignore His message and act like it was never heard
Instead of falling back we need to go forward in life
Will you continue to stumble while we play with the devil's knife
Push yourself forward so you can see the Lord's light
Don't become a victim without even putting up a real fight
Push yourself toward the blessing that is meant for you
Don't allow the enemy to win by the sins he wants you to do
Push away the temptation that will cause you to stray
Take the Lord's hand that was presented to you today
Instead of wandering around blaming all for your pain
Embrace the Lord's path or will you allow His push to be in vain

My Friend

Pull up a chair and please have a seat
While you look around to everyone that your eyes come to meet
When you talk to a stranger that doesn't know you
This will be the beginning of someone without a clue
Now you will have to be open to having a new relationship
Not that you have any idea of where you're heading on this new ship
Sometimes you will get a good feeling while others may feel bad
Yet you rely on your instincts and the signals you've had
Some people start out as friendly while others as a pain
The feeling that you have about this person could really be a strain
Some people become needy while others look for you to lend
When you find a person who is sincere, now this could become a friend
While your guard should remain up and your trust stands firm
Until this person proves themselves, don't allow
them to cause your heart to burn
Life has its lessons that we all need to learn how to respect
This will be the moment that our wall of security begins to reflect
Not everyone will past your great wall of self defense
This will be your moment that your heart builds up its own fence
So one day you will create a test and your golden rule will bend
When this person takes and passes your test
then you will call them your friend

I Got Some Bad News

The phone rang out late last night
While I was asleep it made me feel so uptight
Who could it be that would call me at such an hour
When a voice informed me that I had lost a treasured flower
Please forgive me for calling so late tonight
What I need you to do is understand you will be alright
Tonight the Lord called on one of your loved ones
They went to be in Heaven with the Lord's only son
Wake up my friend and please have a seat
Because this sad news might take away your feet
Please remember that they will always be with you
Know that your love for them was shown by what you do
Hello, hello, are you there, did you hear what I said
The person that you loved so much has just been pronounced dead
Before you act out in any type of way
Just know they will always remember your spirit from yesterday
While your heart sheds a tear and you close your eyes tonight
Just know they left in peace, there wasn't any type of fight
We never know when we will be called,
because it's not a day that we choose
Today is a very sad day because I got some bad news

You Didn't Appreciate Me

Today I went to a funeral and observed a friend cry
Her mother passed away and she simply cried out why
Today I watched my friend breakdown in tears
She was a strange friend who never appreciated all her mother's years
Until you lose someone who was always there for you
Then you will realize how much they did for you
Today this friend cried out "Lord I'm sorry for what I said"
When her mother was alive she always stated
"I can't wait until your dead"
The power in words is something that we just don't understand
Be careful what you say because it can affect any woman or man
While the Lord welcomed her mother in heaven because it was time
While the lady cried out for forgiveness only to
hear the Lord say she is now mines
You didn't appreciate My angel when she was there on earth
So I decided to bring her home where I appreciate everyone's worth
You didn't appreciate My angel when she tried to teach you right
So I've given you what you asked for in the middle of the night
You don't seem to know Me because you never wanted to learn
So I've called My angel home so you can experience the devil's turn
You didn't appreciate all that was given through My grace
So I've decided to leave you alone to enjoy Satan's space

Tears

Tears are a sign of our emotional side
While some try to be strong, others are unable to hide
As a man you are taught that to cry is a sign you're weak
Yet we face this emotion and it leaves us unable to speak
There will come a time when you are faced with a fear
So try to hold back what has been labeled a tear
Some people have weak moments while others just don't wait
Hide this reaction if you must but for some it will be too late
There are tears for a time when we are reminded of pain
How can we stop the emotion that resembles GOD'S rain
Each tear that we shed may be a sign that we care
Some try to hide the fact that they really do care
When your eyes fill with tears yet you refuse to cry
The only real question the Lord ask of you is why?
Own your emotions because they show what your heart hears
Some people can't express how they feel so the Lord gave us tears

What Must I Do

The question was asked by the Lord today
As the church went quiet on this bright sunny day
I've given you life when you didn't deserve
While you felt so entitled I stated you have some nerve
Each day that passed by I gave to you
Yet when I need you to serve, this is something you refuse to do
Each day I wake you up to live another day
Yet you enjoy each moment while forgetting yesterday
Each time you cried out for My helping hand
You promised to serve and replied I understand
So today I watched you cry out without having a clue
Think about the moment, I asked what I must do
Nobody could have promised you another day to breathe
Yet you feel like you're entitled to continue to receive
Think about all you've received without earning anything
Do you realize it's the Lord's love that I bring
So I hope you will be grateful for everything given to you
As the Lord continues to ask what else must I do

Great Expectations

Why the Lord asked do you have great expectations
When you don't deliver any of My given directions
While I give you all that you need
Only to see you destroy with your desires and greed
Stop for a moment and observe what I've given
When you help someone else then you will be forgiven
While you continue to show Me nothing but crumbs
These will be the moments that make My feelings go numb
This will be a moment when the skies turn gray
As the world became scared of My anger today
The Lord cleared His throat and asked what are you expecting
Think about the question while I observe everything
The Lord spoke to me in a very clear voice
Why do you show fear when you're given a choice
There is no limit to whatever I do
Why should I give blessings when I'm ignored by you
I will raise My expectations of what is needed for you to receive
Know your God and show Me you truly believe
I need you to take a moment to see what you've been through
Don't you believe that I was there to walk with you
Take a moment to look back and see all of your life's reflections
Trust in the hand of your GOD as I have great Expectations

Stop Asking The Lord Why

I went to a funeral today of one of my best friends
While I stood over his body, my tears showed me his end
So many people came to give their respect and say goodbye
Yet each person who stepped up could only whisper the word why
Lord why have you come and take away those we care about
While people continued to arrive only so to scream and shout
So many family members, so many friends shaded their tears
When people hear of death they come to visit their own fears
Funny how the people in your life don't ever call or come by to visit
Yet when they hear of a passing, this is a time they care to relive it
A funeral is just a location where all people
come to say their final goodbye
Whether you are family or a friend and some folks don't even know why
Tears will flow today, sadness is almost guaranteed
If we could turn back the hands of time, how far would you need
What would you change in your path to avoid your final day
Don't you realize life is God's plan and you really don't have any say
So don't be upset because your friend is about to go home to Thee
His or her time has come so just be happy
that they are coming home to Me
We all fear the unknown and that's why we don't want to die
Until we arrive at the next stop and then we
can stop asking the Lord why

Dig A Little Deeper

Have you ever thought how far you could go
Until you are pushed to your limit you may never know
Pain and suffering seem to go together hand and hand
The request for more may be hard to understand
You may never get the answer that you truly seek
While your limit may never be reached if you decide to remain weak
The limits you have are only the limits you live by
Dig a little deeper and one day you will reveal why
Most people bend while others give in to pain and break
Yet until you face hard moments you will never find out what it takes
You may one day feel that you have given enough
Yet until you dig a little deeper you really don't understand Mr. Tough
The real toughness, the unreachable brave heart you own
May never be revealed until you answer your guts phone
Just when you feel you must dig a little deeper to win
That will be your moment that your real gut call will begin
Nobody knows the real you until you dig deep inside yourself
Stand up and take a bow because today you discovered your true wealth

Our Father is Upset

Tonight I had a conversation with the Father of us all
While we all seek the Almighty, tonight He answered my call
Every night I would ask the Lord why He chose me
That's when I saw a bright star and heard the voice of Thee
Tonight My son you will have My undivided attention
So pull up a chair and just know you are all My invention
Every sick child, every person who has a heart beat
Was placed here by My hand as I raise all to their feet
Yet each and everyday someone asks what did I bring them here for
My answer is trust in Me is required before you can receive any more
The word called trust is as important as the air you breathe
Without trust in Me how else would I know you are ready to receive
Everyone is placed here for My purpose to be known
This is My world and everyone in it will serve Me until they are grown
Each and every one should know the reflection of My face
They should understand nothing is earned, I give it by My own grace
So before anyone decides to question what I have them do
Just know that I'm the Father of all and that includes you
When I bless anyone, it's because they are given a chance to share
Just know I'm the Father and only I control what happens here
So go out into the world with My children and remember My word
The last days are coming for everyone, so warn them of what you heard

Do You Really Understand?

Tonight I had a conversation with a lady
She reached out to vent and tonight she picked on me
When I answered the phone the lady had a lot to say
Yet she was calm with her voice and I decided to listen today
She wasn't calling to have a simple conversation with me
While her eyes filled with tears she yelled why can't this be
When I asked her to finish what she had to say
Her voice became so direct with anger when she responded "not today"
So I pulled up a chair and began to listen to her story
Why she asked do so many men fail to see the glory
What are you talking about, please be a little clearer than this
That's when she yelled at me and asked please don't make me remiss
So many men ask for a woman's total love and affection
Yet when a woman allows her heart in they
seem to go in a different direction
Why do so many men just want to look at
a woman for her outside beauty
When a woman has to remind her man does he remember me
Why do so many men forget to treat their lady with respect
When the man has her heart it becomes time for her neglect
Why do so many men have chosen a path of cheating
When will he come back to her like he did in the beginning
Why are so many older women left home alone in their bed at night
The response was because they'd rather be
alone instead of the daily fight
I rose up from my chair and told her I cannot speak for every man
She apologized for her outburst and asked do you really understand

A Father's Pain

Today I saw my daughter hold back her pain
As she cried out my man left me in the rain
She had committed herself to love him for many years
Yet today it had ended as she could no longer hold back her tears
While I looked in her eyes and witnessed the sadness in her face
My love is still all I could offer as her hurt needed to be replaced
She confessed that her man had decided to move on
He claimed he needed his own space because he has waited too long
The explanation he gave her would never be enough
Because my little girl loved only him so this was very tough
Everybody goes through pain when their love becomes so deep
I don't know the real reason so my feeling could only label him a creep
While I felt he had another, and wanted to have his own space
All I could remember was my daughter's tears on her face
My daughter never had another love in her entire life
Yet after ten years with this man he never asked her to be his wife
Strange how she allowed this to go on for this long
So when I asked her about his intentions she
would play the same old song
Yet today her world changed and came crashing down
The man that had her heart stated he no longer wanted to be around
Yet my daughter walked away as the clouds brought down her rain
Today was the day she would reveal a father's pain

You Need to Learn

Ladies and gentlemen it's time to pull up a chair
There is so much to learn, while some must experience some fear
The time has come for you to listen and learn
This moment may be too heavy for some
while others will have their turn
Each lesson that you come in contact with may not be easy
Yet while we all have our own growing pains toward destiny
The time will come for you to put your armor down
Take heed to this moment and be grateful you're still around
Each turn that you take has a lesson deep inside
Until you pay full attention to the process, all you can do is hide
While you go through the jungle that we all consider a maze
How else do you think you can survive these troubled days
Each time that you take a step on the path you believe is right
Only to discover that you're never alone in the middle of the night
Each journey that you have taken was because of your choice
How do you think you made it without hearing GOD'S voice
Your steps were already chosen and yet doubt still is within you
What will it take before you realize what you're meant to do
So trust in the Lord and your steps will become clear at every turn
Put down your shield of doubt because you have so much to learn

The Lord's Eye Test

Today I heard a sermon that touched my soul
While I listened to the words that my heart was told
The bishop sat us down and explained his own eye test
While I listened to his sermon, there came a breeze from the west
Now let's take a moment to observe what you have received
The Lord sat me down and gave me a reality check
While so many complain only to become a nervous wreck
Pull up a chair because the whole world needs to sit down
The time has come for you to realize that life's
problems can make you frown
Let's begin your eye test because My son you really need to see
What if you only had what you've earned in life, were would you be
Take a look at what you have, did you earn anything
Let's adjust the lens to see exactly what you
have that your hands did bring
The time has come for Me to address everyone
who has a need to complain
I want you all to understand that with My
blessings there will be some pain
Let's switch seats and I want you to sit in My chair
Would you be as forgiving to everyone, do
you think you would really care
Now I want you to take· a look at all that I have given you
Can you think of anything that you required Me to do
Now look through the lens and tell me is it
better with Me or without Me
Think about your answer before you make
the mistake of letting Satan be
Take another moment and remember that
I am waiting for you to confess
I hope you can clearly see My blessing of you,
or will you fail the Lord's eye test

Thank You For

Who are you and why do you feel you're owed anything
Take a moment to look in a mirror to discover what you bring
Who are you to complain about what you may want
Do you really have a need or is it just something for you to flaunt
Who are you to ask for something else to waste
Do you really feel lucky enough to receive the devil's hungry taste
So many times you call out for things you don't deserve
Take a minute to discover that fact; you really have a lot of nerve
How would you like to get a taste of what you would be
Do you really want to test the waters without
your one and only MOMMY
How would you like to be shown life based on your childish actions
Are you ready for me to point out your mistakes
while you cause all your distractions
You want to complain, you really want to break
things, and you want to cry out
Let me know when you're ready for me to flip
the coin so you can really shout
Your time is running out, you're wearing out your welcome mat
Do you really want me to walk away, make you
homeless, can you really handle that
Stop your nonsense and look at life through your own reality
Otherwise you may lose the life of comfort I
provide and become your own casualty
Learn to appreciate what you have because it can all be taken away
Once you lose things and people you love, the empty
feeling will be a reminder of yesterday
Stop the destruction by causing the ones who love you so much pain
Because where the world sees you heading,
you really have nothing to gain
We know you're smart, and it's clear you understand what to do
Instead of acting out and blaming everyone else,
how about just saying thank you.

My Gratitude Letter

This is a letter that you may never expect
While I write these words for you as my true suspect
Because you are my father, the man who never left me
Even if I didn't agree with the way you let my life be
While I struggled at times and questioned
the method, I didn't understand
The lessons that I learned from you prepared me to become a strong man
While I cried at night, complained during the
day, these actions fell on deaf ears
Little did I realize that you were preparing me to
become a strong man for many years
Even when some people would ask where is your daddy now
Today I can say he has made me what I am
and my spirit can yell out WOW
While most people just look at themselves and wonder why
Yet when I questioned your words of wisdom,
that's when my spirit would cry
Don't get me wrong, there were many times I felt hate for you
Because being a child and accepting your wisdom wasn't easy to do
We are all seeds that need to be planted so we can grow
Children are only offspring that have no clue of where to go
So thank you for my lessons that you have instilled in me
Thank you for the fact that your wisdom has allowed me to be
Thank you for the good times, the bad times and for most of all
Staying in my life with our protection and not allowing me to fall
When the Lord placed me under your golden wing
Never did anyone expect to witness or
understand the love you could bring
So Dad, I now understand you did your best for me
How can anyone judge you without finding themselves guilty?

Your Yesterday

Now pull up a chair because you'll need to sit down
The Lord spoke to me and he wasn't fooling around
Everyone who lives has their own yesterday
So did you spend your own time to kneel down and pray
When Thee spoke to me he seemed very upset with us all
Nobody is excluded from the Lord when he makes the final call
The first question he asked was how dare you ignore me
Do you all remember the times you called out to THEE
The second question he asked was why do you feel you don't have to pray
Do you remember that panic or fear you had expressed only yesterday
The third question he asked was do you
think you've made it on your own
Do you remember when you felt fear and I
reminded you that you're never alone
Now these are samples for you to think about and trust I have more
Do you get the picture I'm painting or should I shut your door
Would you like me to remain angry because I do have another side
Yesterday can be a sample of the pain you caused me to hide
Would you like me to bring down my anger in pain
The last time I did that it was forty days of my rain
Learn from yesterday because it is only a part of your past
The lessons that I give are so that you won't have to ask
Just know who I am and it all begins when you learn to pray
Remember my words everyone or I will remind you of your yesterday

Your Mask

While we wake up each morning with a new day to face
Never considering what blessings were given by God's grace
We rise from the bed just thinking of the new day
While we expect everything to simply be okay
Now everybody has problems that they have to deal with
Some handle life with ease and while others wait for theirs to shift
Now when you face the world to tackle any task
Do you show your true colors or put on your own mask
While not everyone can handle the road that they travel
Are you ready to start your own adventure where anything can unravel
Can you admit that each day may bring a new fear
Then you should realize that everyone has their own reason to be here
Instead of worrying about what could happen to you every day
Just pray every morning and ask the Lord to guide your way
The path that you're placed on will be given without any fear
Just know that he is with you and show that you're willing to hear
Each step that you take is because the Lord gave you the ability
Just know your trust will guide you with your faith in Thee
While you face each day just know he will answer any question you ask
Because today is a new day that you can smile without your mask

Fellas

Now fellas I need you to hear the ladies out
While some may fail to admit what I'm talking about
Pull up a chair and please take a seat
While the ladies have become a voice that has turned up the heat
Fellas I've heard the ladies venting just how they feel
Even as they dress to impress with their own sex appeal
Don't get it twisted because they are more than you see
Women are creatures of habit who want to show their own beauty
I took time to listen to what the women of today had to say
They feel men act like it's only about sex and
that remains their focus of today
Fellas, the ladies have spoken and have made themselves clear
They want more than a show because they
are much more than "yes dear"
Fellas they want to know that they are much more than sex
Can you offer them anything else or are they just another text
Instead of running a game or trying to get in every lady's bed
Try listing to her heart and responding to the feelings that you're fed
Fellas you're in a ball game and it's time to step up to the plate
While some may promise you their world, others
may not be worthy of another date
Fellas we are all guilty of looking and admiring another man's girl
Yet how far would you go if she revealed her real world
Take a moment fellas to look at the girl by your side
Have you been blessed or is she someone you may want to hide
Fellas take your time to find the mate who will complete you
Because if you look really close you might discover you never had a clue

Grace Of Today

Do you know how often the Lord came to you
Yet he was turned away because you didn't have a clue
The real question is, do you truly believe he exist
Wishing for a miracle yet your spirit wasn't having any of this
Each day you wake up expecting to have another day
Do you realize not everyone was blessed in that same way
How many times did you feel goosebumps arise
Why was this just a moment that came as a surprise
So many try to avoid the Holy Spirit in their lives every single day
While the Lord still provides them with a chance to pray
The Lord continues to reach out and hopes that we will listen
But it isn't until he shows his anger when
people decide to become a Christian
The love of the Lord scares so many because they never can comprehend
They question how someone could love me
more than my own best friend
This was the moment that the sun shined through the cloudy skies
The voice was so strong it brought tears to my eyes
My child understand me because I want to be crystal clear
While you wander on the earth just know I can still hear
My child you have been blessed every single day
Look around at what you have because not
everyone can remember yesterday
My son you seem to forget that I'm your father and you are my child
Understand what you have before I take away your smile
When you take a moment and realize it can all be taken away
That will be your defining moment of your given grace of today

The Tears On My Face

I woke up this morning with tears on my face
Not knowing why these tears visited my space
Then I had a vision of the times with you Mommy
As the vision of my past times began to overtake me
Since the day my mother passed on I was reminded of her hand
The vision with her smile brought tears that now I began to understand
Mommy you will always be the rock that built me
This was the moment that I began to understand
the true meaning of Mommy
Each day that you tried to teach me the meaning of wrong from right
Was another day that your little man put up his own fight
While never understanding your reasons that made you cry
The little man wasn't ready to answer to your question why
Never did the little man think that one day
he would become a grown man
Because his mother covered him with so much
love that he just couldn't understand
While his mother did all she could to show him her own grace
She would always say son you need to listen to
my words before I leave this place
Now the day has come for me to go on and let you be on your own
The Lord has called me home and it's time for you to be grown
Mommy please don't leave me alone in this scary place
That was the moment when I had awakened with tears on my face

Finding You

Today I met a man who had come to his own terms
While he spoke of his life, he still had a lot to learn
The man was surrounded by his family and friends
Yet when he told his story about himself, happily it had no end
This man was on vacation on a cruise ship in the big blue sea
Yet he had an inner spirit that wanted to be free
While the ship floated around without any land in sight
He was so anxious to get home and that just didn't seem right
Finally he broke down and said this vacation isn't really for me
Yet the Lord kept him close because he needed this time at sea
The man had all he wanted, fancy cars, a
nice house and plenty of money
Yet he really wasn't happy because of his inner
life which didn't include Thee
While he gave things to so many and was
surrounded by plenty of friends
He still had time to think back to his good times from way back when
As he explained his love for bikes and fancy cars
The Lord wouldn't allow his focus to go but so far
So I asked him what is wrong, what else do you need
As he pondered my question, he answered by saying it's not greed
My heart and mind seem to be all over the place
While he spoke of family and friends you could see hurt in his face
He said I'm very happy with my life and grateful for family
But the hurt inside my heart doesn't allow the spirit to be free
The answer was clear and I will tell you what you must do
Take time away from your family and friends
because you need to first find you

Hello You

I want everyone to take a minute and look inside
Find the real you that we all want to hide
Now this might not be such an easy thing to do
That will take some courage to say "hello you"
While we go about our business pretending everything is okay
Do you really feel comfort in living life this way
When you take time to really pay attention to what we do
Then we have to ask the question, did you say "hello you"
We all have times in our lives that we seem to regret
While we live in the moment that we all rather forget
While we grow older and think of our own memories
Do you ever wonder how we allowed ourselves these miseries
When we rethink all the wild and crazy things we use to do
Sometimes we laugh or maybe cry, but did we ever say "hello you"
Do you ever feel as we grow older these thoughts should go away
Yet we still remember our past like it was yesterday
Can you forgive, will they forget, or did you decide to run
What do you remember about yesterday other that having fun
Just take a moment and think back as you take a real look within
As you start to realize the pain or the thrill
that comes from where you've been
Just think about what you lived through and
witness the impact on what you do
Have you learned from your past, if so then it's time to say "hello you"

The Interview

Hello everyone who thinks they are all alone
Let me inform you that not all calls are answered by a telephone
The day will come in time for both me and for you
When the Lord our father will reach out and
conduct your personal interview
While you're here on earth living the life you should cherish
The day will come when the world will see you perish
As people gather to say their final thoughts and goodbyes
Some will mourn the loss while others will scream and cry
Yet despite if you believe that everyone will see this day
Only those worthy of the Holy Spirit will be welcomed in a heavenly way
The only question that will come as the Lord prepares for you
Will you be ready for the most important scheduled interview
Now this moment is a big one because you will be asked to testify
You will be so nervous as the first question asked will be WHY
My child why have you forsaken me when I stood by you
As your tears begin to flow, his voice will question what will you do?
My child don't tremble, don't panic because it's now too late
Nobody ever knows me until they reach my pearly gate
My child when did I leave your side, when were you ever without me
Haven't I always responded in my time yet you wouldn't listen to THEE
Yet you claim Lord I didn't understand or know what to do
Just remember my warning because you will
need to prepare for your final interview

Are You Ready To Fight

There comes a time when you need to make a stand
This is a moment for every woman and every man
The flesh has desires that are hard to resist
Yet we submit to the temptation because we enjoy all of this
Each year brings a time that we are reminded to fast for 40 days
Can you do without giving into the devil's
temptations that will make you sway
This call on your spirit will be a challenge of each night
That's when the Holy Spirit will ask are you ready to fight
Denial is something that will test how strong you are
Temptation will rise up to test your spirit to push you so far
When you deny the flesh, when you deny temptation's call
The real question is are you ready to fight or are you ready to fall
The call will be loud because you are being tempted to pick a side
Is temptation your choice or will you stand up with some pride
So many people make a choice that they never are able to keep
Only to witness they have failed again at a
promise that makes them weep
Why do you bother to make a promise that you know you will break
How would you feel if the Lord put your word on the give and take
When will you stand up to the devil's challenge and say not tonight
Put on your boxing gloves and answer the
call by saying "I'm ready to fight"

Good Morning Pain

Every day I awaken from the night before
Each time the moment comes when you're leaving out my front door
It's the pain of you leaving me; me alone from you
This makes my heart cry out what will my emotions do
Good morning pain as I search the skies for the rain
While I ask for forgiveness of everybody's pain
Hurt can run deep and yet it is felt by most
Wondering what did I do as my pain is felt from coast to coast
Help me this morning to understand this feeling that's felt so deep inside
Lord can you please explain this hurt that I try to hide
Good morning pain comes when you carry pain form last night
Waking up to another day only to face the pain and his fright
Good morning pain I was hoping that you would go away
Hear my words as I continue to feel this pain for another day
Last night while I laid my head down to sleep
Praying for the Lord to bless me as I wondered would I ever keep
Yet the Lord blessed me with another clear sunny day
As I rose to my feet that's when I realized I needed to pray
Good morning pain, why are you still hear in my space
What have I done to allow your hurt to replace my grace
At that moment I felt the tears on my face from Thee
You have allowed pain to replace the touch of me
Face your guilt and remove his hands from your heart
Today is a new day for your spirt as you say good morning to a fresh start

Do You Remember Me

Today is a happy day because I'm heading home
While I won't see any of you my spirit won't be alone
I'm happy that you have spread the word about my leaving
While the crowds gathered today I observed the angels begin to sing
My spirit is in heaven now but you can bet I will be watching
Come as you are my family and friends but
make sure it's happiness you bring
Find a stranger today and tell them your name
Become someone special today and know
that your life won't be the same
We all have a past that has its own memories
Yet I hope that you have learned from all of these
Not every person you know is someone you enjoyed
But nobody will ever know if they are an angel who has been deployed
The funeral today is a special moment for all to see
While your eyes fill with tears of our own special memories
My last request will be a simple one yet I still must ask
Turn to the person next to you and say knowing you has been a blast
Give them a hug and tell them your entire name
While the clouds cover the skies, just know today isn't a shame
I hope that each and every one has said a prayer to Thee
My final question to you is DO you remember ME

Where Are You At?

The morning is the beginning of everyone's day
Yet we never seem to remember the blessings of yesterday
While most people expect to have another day to live
Do they ever think about who or what they will have to give
Take a moment out of your day and look to the sky
Say thank you to your father instead of asking the question why
Just think about the last time trouble visited you
When you didn't have an answer to what you needed to do
Each time you were faced with a problem you couldn't solve
How many of your so called friends refused to get involved
When you were faced with a problem or suffered a great loss
Each time you refused your Lord he still kept you on his course
What will it take before you wake up and smell the Lord's coffee
Do you really want the Lord to make an example of you for all to see
Even the strongest man or woman can be humbled at any time
Don't make your father angry to the point
that he will commit an awful crime
The day will come when he will close every
path you might decide to take
This will be the beginning of your path to a very costly mistake
Just know your place and remember he has always had your back
Think about this before he ask where are you at?

My Today

Today I have the Lord to be grateful to
Because without his grace I wouldn't know what to do
Today he lifted me up so that I could have another day
Yet so many fail to drop down to their knees to begin to pray
Today I must learn that tomorrow isn't a guarantee
While there are so many reasons to be grateful to Thee
Today I must learn to be grateful for my tears
Because they are a reminder that I didn't have to be here
Today I must learn that all I have is his gift
Too many forget the Lord's love as their spirits continue to drift
Today I must help a stranger with my own gifted hand
Too many forget that Jesus forgave those when they didn't understand
Today when I look to heaven and ask the Lord why
My father looked down and said because they made my son cry
Today when I seek the Lord for his love and advice
He has always answered me without thinking twice
Today will be the first day that I find someone to forgive
That's when I heard the Lord's voice say
"Now you understand how to live"
Today will be the day that I prayed for someone else's sorrow
That's when the Lord smiled at me and said
my son I will see you tomorrow
While I kneeled down and began to pray
That's when the Lord reminded me about my own Today

The Lord Asked Where Are You At?

I called on you in my time of need
Yet instead of an answer you turned away my greed
When I asked for you to come to my aide
Yet instead of your assistance I felt your presence begin to fade
I wondered when you would respond to my call
Yet instead of your support you allowed me to fall
How could I ever believe in the one known as Thee
When I called on your support you never came to me
That's when a rumble came from a clear blue sky
Startled by this all happening made tears fill my eyes
The time had come when I was confronted by the Lord
You have made several statements that you really can't afford
My sons, My daughters let me set this record straight
Every time I called on your spirit, your response to me was to wait
Each time that you had a problem that you couldn't solve
Your trust in Thee was something you allowed to dissolve
Each moment in your walk met bumps on your road
Yet instead of humbling your steps it was anger you would unload
So the next time you come before me with any complaints about Thee
Remember who you're addressing instead of asking how this could be
Instead of asking questions you need to remember that
Each time I responded with my own question, "Where are you at?"

I Called Out To You

Today I heard a voice and it really scared me
While the voice was so powerful it stated I am Thee
YES it's in the middle of the night because I want your attention
Who is this that you follow or are you too afraid to mention
Today you heard my commands yet you decided to stray
When you were questioned by my angel you answered not today
Who are you that you can simply turn away from me
No matter what you want in life just know that it comes through Thee
Each time you were spoken to by me you turned a deaf ear
So I decided to take away another blessing to show you real fear
Each time you complained this task seems to be impossible
You needed my lesson of faith so I chose to make you responsible
Each struggle you faced was another lesson from THEE
Only I could stop your pain because it was I who caused your misery
Learn my children from the path that only I can choose
As long as you deny me this will be a path that you will surly lose
I am the father and you will listen to me or surly die
Know who I am because the Lord is King and you will understand why
I am your father and children will learn to worship me
This will be my final warning before you feel the wrath of Thee
When you question me, you will kneel down and ask what must I do
You will remember this day that your GOD called out to you

You're Never Alone

Everyone has a moment when they have the fear of being alone
This will be the time when most people will reach out for the telephone
Not everyone has somebody that they can reach out to
Yet these times come more often than anyone wants to admit too
Take this moment to pray to the Lord and express how you feel
These times may sound empty but you can rest assured GOD is real
The Lord knows your spirit, he hears us when we cry
Never judging our pain when we all have a moment to question why
Everyone has hard times when they can't seem to find a way
Happy moments and hard times will be life in the Lord's way
Yet no matter the problem we seem to find out what to do
Did you really think your father would ever abandon you
Each step that you take is followed by another
Just think of how lonely your steps would be without each other
You have two hands so that one hand will give while the other can serve
To think that you're too big to help someone, boy you have a lot of nerve
Each day that you move forward in life is a day the Lord will atone
Just remember we are all his children and we are never alone

I'm Ready To Fight

As I woke up last night with sweat on my face
There was anger in my spirit that I had to replace
Each second that went by was simply time that I wasted
When I think of the moment of the hate that I tasted
I'm ready to fight for the Holy Spirit within me
So why is Satan testing my devotion to Thee
While Satan stood up and made me a promise of his own
Come follow me and enjoy the world that I truly own
The ladies, the money and the rest of this world will be in your hands
I'll promise you whatever you want if you just follow my plans
The Lord you have listened to is no match for me
Come follow my road to paradise and forget about Thee
The Lord you remember as a little lost child
Hasn't been seen by anyone in such a long while
Yet I am here and the devil makes his claim to you tonight
The question Satan wants answered is do you know what is right
Take another moment and look around far and near
When you have a desire, whose voice do you hear
The Lord you worship keeps telling you everything is alright
Yet will you walk with Satan or did the Lord tell you I'm ready to fight

The Real Family

Today we came together to talk as a family
We put aside our personal feelings to talk freely
Today we had to address a family problem at hand
So we put aside the pride and spoke as family that would understand
Today we formed a circle so we could feel as one
The feelings we have felt needed to be revealed by everyone
How long have we held back from our own hidden truth
When would we reveal the pain that was hidden like a bad tooth
Who would take the first step toward our much needed healing
Can we grow together as one by starting our own believing
Not everyone who is called on will be able to take the lead
The time has come for the family to address some of our needs
Every family member will have the floor to address their own concerns
Yet this moment wasn't created for us to dish
any dirt, it was meant for all to learn
How long will we live a lie by saying everything is okay
When our spirit knows the truth to finally yell out not today
Until we all move on from the past and accept who we really are
This cloud that hangs over family won't allow anyone to go very far
But when we forgive the past and allow all the hidden hurt to go free
That will be the moment when we can all become a real family

I Can't Cry For You

Today I received a call from my daughter
Kimberly who had a troubled past
While I listen to her problems, I realized my patience couldn't last
She complained about her mother, she complained about her brother
Yet when I began to understand her pain, I
realized there wasn't any other
My daughter had her problems just like anyone else her age
When I began to pay attention to her story, that's
when I realized that she lived in her own cage
My daughter stayed away from her family because she felt so all alone
Yet when she became so depressed she would reach
out to her older sister on her telephone
She tried to get herself help, she joined a
clinic, and she found new friends
Yet after about two months of trying these
things she put these efforts to an end
One day my daughter called on the telephone and
said I've decided to go back to school
Daddy would you come to class with me so I don't become a class fool
My daughter got upset when I told her that I
cannot do this favor that you ask
There are many things that I can do but
believe me this wouldn't be my task
She began to cry, daddy how can I ever learn
or get to spend time with you

That's when I explained to her that there're
somethings in life that I just can't do
She cried out why won't you help me, my mother
never gave me a rightful chance
That's when I explained to her that she did the
best she could even with her last dance
Pull yourself together and become the lady that you were meant to be
How will you ever learn from your mistakes in
life when you won't ever listen to me
There are many things you can do once you
put an effort toward your goals
What may seem like a heavy task can be obtained
if you listen to what you're told
So get your act together and try to focus on what you need to do
There are many things you must learn, but I need
you to understand that I won't cry for you

Selfish

Good morning everyone who believes they aren't selfish
When you are confronted by the question only to answer I'm not this
Maybe you're not but let's take a look at the real you
Would you accept this title given by others who watch what you do
While you feel you are kind and give to those only you want
The question is do you only help others so that you can flaunt
Have you ever helped a stranger because you knew of their pain
The question becomes clear, if you did so only for your own gain
Just remember this is your trip and you may have been accused
Do you only look out for yourself because at some point you got used
When you help someone just think about your real intention
This may have a hidden agenda that you failed to mention
This trip might be painful when you look into the real light
Did you realize that the selfish one lives within you tonight
It's never too late to change and show others you can begin to care
The question is are you ready to change or remain every one's beware
To be a selfish person could have some past hurt within you
We have to ask point blank what you are willing to do
Once you discover Mr. or Ms. Selfish, will
you say I don't want any of this
Or will you remain the one known to all as Mr. or Ms. SELFISH.

A Wedding Vow

Not too long ago we met and our eyes teared
While we enjoyed our vision only to sample fear
Attracted for a moment as my heart skipped a beat
My vision blurred as I stumbled to a smile that our hearts would greet
Hello pretty lady can you please tell me your name
While you hesitated to answer because you felt this was a game
Finally you told me as you looked me up and down
Did I pass your inspection as my jaw hit the ground
You smiled at me once before you answered my question
With tears in your eyes you apologized for the hesitation
When you finally told me your name with tears in your eyes
Out of concern I responded why you are so surprised
We agreed we should take this moment to freeze our time
As I felt so elated to be able to dream of you as mine
Let's learn each other because we need to get this moment right
We need to talk and trust so we can claim our feelings tonight
When you feel you have met the person who could be your wife
Don't take things at face value but consider her yours for life
There will be problems, the pain may become very strong
How will we ever make this work if we don't test right and wrong
So let's take a chance and take what some call a leap
Our time together has shown that our love will keep
Throw all the fears away, let's remember when we both said WOW
Today we have to acknowledge our own personal wedding vows

I Didn't Know

Hello everyone who thinks they know everything
Are you really prepared for what the world will bring
Have you lived your life believing you know it all
Just to be humbled when you received the Lord's call
When you wake up from the blessing of a good night sleep
Did you know the Lord watched over your soul to keep
While you spend your day facing people you never seen before
Do you realize that person could be someone who opens your new door
When you called out for help in the middle of the night
Only to find the Lord's tears showing you things will be alright
While you go through your days putting on a strong face
Did you know the Lord prepared your path
with a blessing already in place
When you meet a stranger who shows you
something you don't understand
Maybe it could be an angel sent to reveal GOD'S plan
While you cry out in anger or feel you need
to face the world with disgust
Why do you feel so disappointed when your chosen path is a must
Take a leap of faith and stop believing your sight
When you gave yourself to the Lord, didn't he say you would be alright
Did you know your life has already been written in stone
So please tell me why you feel you are all alone
Since you feel you really don't know where or why you need to go
Maybe your real answer to life is to stop saying I didn't know

The Hand Of Thee

Lord, each time I called on you the results were the same
When I had a problem it was my spirit that had to learn
While my heart would feel the disappointment followed by pain
As I felt so abandoned by the reach that was delayed in the rain
The water from the skies made me begin to breakdown and cry
Yet as life would continue to show me the real reason why
Lord each time I looked for you to come and help me out
You stood by in heaven only to make me figure it all out
Where is the father who claimed to always be by my side
Why is it time to turn away from my rescue when pain rests inside
Lord each time my eyes would fill up with painful tears
What may seem like moments have turned into painful years
So today I decided that I would stop seeking you
This is the only thing left that I feel that I can do
Suddenly the clouds would block the sun from my face
Coldness came on a summer morning without leaving a trace
Suddenly I heard a voice that was so deep but stern
Son you haven't been listening; son will you ever learn
Just because you don't see me doesn't mean I went away
Each problem you encounter is my lesson for another day
While you grow impatient about what you need from me
How can you ever survive without trusting the hand of Thee

Hello My Heart

Hello my heart, can I have a moment of your time
As I think of our moments in the past you're what makes me shine
You have been beating inside of me every step of the way
So before I take another moment for granted,
I choose to thank GOD today
Each morning my eyes open, each breath that I continue to take
I'm so grateful for another day an pray I'm forgiven for any mistake
Hello my heart, can I have another moment to say thank you
Because without your strength I wouldn't know what to do
So I look to the sky and bow my head with your grace
Only to be humbled by my Lord with tears on my face
Each problem that I face isn't a real problem at all
While I trust in the Lord's word that reminds
me that he won't allow me to fall
Hello my heart I want to thank you for lifting my spirit
Even when I fail you it's only because I refuse to hear it
Each time I call on you to show me your way
There is your voice inside of me that I have come to trust today
Hello my heart there is no place I would rather be
So I thank you my Lord for blessing a wretch like me

The Lost And Found Of A Man

Ladies I want you to listen to me
The information I'm about to give you will set your mind free
While many ladies have lost their man to another lady
Did you ever consider the fact that maybe you are shady
Now don't get upset by what I'm about to tell you
Just listen for a minute while I try to get you through
Most men approach a woman that has captured their attention
While he goes into his approach, I'm sure
there are things he didn't mention
Not every man will expose his whole life to just anyone
Yet you have taken his mind to a place which is much more than just fun
When you first met the person that you became attracted to
Did you ever question the person when they questioned you
The moves, the lines, the energy that you gave from the start
What happened to that person, did you forget to do your part
Have you become so comfortable that your loving no longer exist
Yet now you complain that he has changed, whose fault is this
Then you meet the lady who has taken your place
While she smiles because she found your
man, as she now enjoys your space
Don't get mad at the man who loved your loving ways
When you changed your efforts an chased your man away
There are many people who are willing to take your place
They are looking in the lost and found of a man with empty space

What's Your Memory?

We all have moments that we wish we could remember
Whether it's today or yesterday, either June or September
While our memory is all that we have to live for
How could we ever live in the moment yet ask for even more
This time or next time are all turned to a memory
Yet we continue to live on asking how this could be
Through hard times and easy moments we try to live right
While we wonder how could our happy days turn into scary nights
When you think back to a moment some will bring a smile
So which of your moments brings you to act like a child
Not every moment brings you to a happy moment in your past
Can you think back to when you felt that our happiness couldn't last
Cherish each day and be grateful when they are great
Take a moment you regret as you're granted a clean slate
Not everyone will be able to say thank you for getting a new way
Did you ever think you would be given a chance for a new today
Rise up from your day because we aren't promised another
Help all who you can whether they are your sister or your brother
The Lord has delivered you from the devil's
hands and allowed you to see
Live in the moment and remember the blessed times of your memory

Pride Vs Trust

Today I went to a class for ladies and gentleman
Yet as I looked around there was a look of concern from all of them
While everyone was asked "can they get ready to trust?"
This was a class about their relationships,
which seemed to alarm all of us
The speaker revealed that we will have to put aside our pride tonight
Can you put away your pride because it may become a terrible fight
Stand in a line with your hands on the person's shoulder in front
While everyone did as they were asked to complete this stunt
You will be led by the leader with your eyes closed all the time
Take each step with the trust of the person ahead of the line
We were led down a hallway without being able to see
Trusting the lead of the person in front of the line representing THEE
Blindly we followed without ever being able to see our destination
Yet before we had taken a single step there was a lot of hesitation
After taking a few steps we knew we could trust our leader
No matter what path that was taken we all followed him or her
The lesson we learned became so clear toward the end
If you can trust another person whom is a stranger then why not a friend
So the question is "can you put aside all of your pride?"
Trust the Lord's path that you have seemed to push aside
Before you can claim that you can give the Lord your trust
Try to put away your pride because the first step is a must!

Why Should I Help Another

Today I walked down a street and was approached by a man
All of the people walking by this stranger
and yet I could fully understand
Each step that I had taken was a moment set up by Thee
How the Lord gave me another one of his own opportunities
While I walked down this street observing several strangers in need
What if the role was reversed I thought,
needing help of my mouth to feed
When you take the time to think about what life could be
That should be the moment you should be
grateful of your own life from Thee
So many people would change places with what the Lord has given you
Just to have what you throw away and we all know that this is true
There are so many organizations that provide help or some type of relief
Yet because our coldness has gotten to a point
that we have become the real thief
Look around you and see how people suffer in every type of way
Please tell me how you would feel if all of a
sudden life treated you this way
When you see a stranger asking for food and a little change, or anything
Just take a moment to consider what a little kindness could surely bring
Hopefully one day you will realize that what has
been given can surely be taken away
Those homeless, less fortunate people you
meet didn't always live this way
When you turn away and judge someone because of how they look
Think about who you are and when you didn't
have and tell me who's the crook
Your mission in life if you decide to accept
should be to help who you can
Learn to accept your blessing as you begin to truly understand
When you see that stranger on the street who
could be your sister or brother
That will be your answer as to why you should help another

Let's Make Things Right!

Today I watched a television show that brought me to tears
It was about a doctor who wanted to make a difference and erase all fear
He was new to this hospital and he arrived late one night
No one knew his intentions as he yelled, "Let's make things right."
Too many policies and too many old rules
The time has come for us to fire all the fools
No more policies that restrict us from saving lives
When faced with a problem we will do all we can and never give up
The first call will be to all those who don't believe
They will be fired because it is our patients we care about
They deserve all of your attention and are to be your first concern
This will be the new policy that will be put into place
So if you can't abide by this, please rest assured
You will be fired first and I will be the one showing you the door
There is a new way to operate and we will do all we can
No matter how rich or poor
No matter if you are a woman or man
This hospital is here to help everyone who is in need
No longer will policy stop you from being doctors and I hope you agree
Today is a new day and if you don't agree with me tonight
Tell me any problems; let's make things right!

Mama Please!

Today I had to take my time so I could remember the sad occasion
Everyone sat and cried out about last November
My mama's life had come to a sudden end
That was also the time I lost my closest friend
Tears flowed down my saddened face
I witnessed that there wasn't a dry eye in the whole place
Some people stood up, others fell to their knees
All I could do was scream out loud, "Mama please"
You never know when someone's time will come to an end
All you can do is remember them and their lasting effects
As you think back over your times together whether good or bad
You realize how special that person was and the place they held
Today you only have your memories to hold on to
Sad for a life taken too soon and because our loved one has left us
All we can do is fall to our knees and break down and cry
Let's all stand and raise a glass as collectively we say, "Mama please!"

Couldn't Sleep Last Night!

When people lay down to finally rest
Do they really know whether or not they will awaken
Will they ever pass God's test
We complete our tasks each day and wonder if it was the Lord's agenda
Do you ever go over the details as you try to remember
You close your eyes trusting that you will awaken each morning after
You trust in the Lord while others feel they are forsaken
Why do some people have a restless night tossing and turning
Do you remember each day's lesson? If so, do you put them into practice
As we each live and breathe mistakes are inevitable
Do we reflect on our mishaps, missteps and
our actions; do we bother to pray
How many times has the Lord given you everything including grace
So why do you continue to fail Him when
all He asks you is for first place
Allow the Lord to work himself into your heart so he can use you
How long will you fight His will, how long
will you run and refuse to serve Him
You wonder why the Lord comes to you in the middle of the night
That's because you don't listen when He
calls before you are ready to fight
You toss, turn; you struggle and tell yourself it will be alright
Then you wonder why you couldn't sleep last night!

It Wasn't Me

Today I had to admit "It wasn't me" was nothing but an excuse
The Holy Spirit asked, "have you trusted in me"?
So many people seek the Lord only in their time of need
Can you honestly say you live the life of a Christian or the life of greed
When the devil tempts you to do something that you know is wrong
How many times have you surrendered to his
temptation or was it too strong
When you're in a moment of denial and you blame the powers that be
How often did you yell out the words "Lord it wasn't me"
When you try to fight temptation and come before the Lord
Why didn't you trust your father instead of saying you couldn't afford
Why do you feel ashamed to show the world you trust in Thee
Yet when you're asked why by your God you
still claim Lord "it wasn't me"
While you live your life and your true spirit is exposed
Each time you were asked to follow the Lord's way
that was another time to turn up your nose
Despite all that you've done you are still forgiven because you are chosen
The blessings promised for you were put on
hold just as your heart is frozen
When you are asked are you ready for the promised
blessing what will your answer be
That's when another lie came out by you answering Lord it wasn't me
So the Lord reviewed your life pointing out every turn you took
Each time he questioned your actions he
reminded you of the Good Book
Finally the Lord asked for your answer to the charges brought up to Thee
Yet all you could do was continue to lie and say "Lord, it wasn't me"

The Trial

We all live here on this planet called Earth
Do we really understand our own true worth
There was a trial in Heaven that was called to order
The devil challenged God to determine if
the earth should be slaughtered
So the Lord called out to the planet known to all as Earth
To ask for a witness who was blessed from its own birth
Who could come forward and defend their man's actions
Who could stand up and be judged to the Lord's satisfaction
While the devil called out to everyone that his demons knew
The trial seemed to favor Satan because he knew exactly what to do
Each person on earth had been guilty for committing a sin
Each and every one was put on trial knowing that they couldn't win
The trial went on and there wasn't much of a defense
Each person that was questioned had committed their own offense
One by one the people lined up only to be shot down
Satan merely smiled with his silly grin like Bozo the clown
The closing arguments gave Satan the upper hand
That's the moment the Lord stepped in to defend every guilty man
The Lord yelled, "Enough is enough"
While the Lord knew this trial would definitely be tough
Satan, you are right about the things that were spoken today
Yet I am the judge and I've allowed things to get this way
Nobody is perfect Satan and that also includes you
This trial proves man needs more of me and
I will be watching what they do

Suffer No More

Today is the day everyone will be forgiven
So stand up my children and see how you are living
As you stand here today on this planet called Earth
I forgive you all because the Lord knows your worth
Let your tears flow, let your hurt be released
As I cleanse your soul and release the fear of the beast
Each and every one of you has a cross to bear
Stop trying to be the one who claims that you don't care
The time has come for your spirit to soar and be free
As you stand before your father today I want
you to feel the blessings of Thee
Now each of you must confess that you are ready to be forgiven
As you tremble before me, this will be your
moment to change how you're living
I am a jealous GOD and I want you to listen to no other
I've allowed you to live a long happy life without judging one another
Stand up my children because you all have a lot of work to do
Pay attention and obey my words as they are revealed to you
If you continue to forsake me and stay on your current path
Then you leave me no choice but to bring upon the world my own wrath
So do yourself a favor and accept my warning before I close my door
Only then will you receive my favor and suffer no more

Why Have You Forgotten Me?

Do you have a parent who lives in a nursing home
Think about the moments they are left all alone
Do you remember the days when you were a child
That same person did all they could to see you smile
Now they are old and can no longer help you out
Why have you decided to abandon the one that only screamed and shout
Each day that they spend alive, left alone in their bed
This is a shame because they always made sure that you were fed
Yet they lay down another day spent at the hands of strangers
Wondering why you have abandoned them in the hands of danger
The sun rises each day as they open their eyes
Do you remember the times that you told them your lies
While you had a need or a desire, they helped you out
Now the need for your company has come and they can only shout
As they are placed in a home under a strangers care
Only to feel abandoned because your voice is no longer there
They wait on the Lord to take them so they can live and be set free
The final question their tears ask is "Why have you forgotten me?"

A New Day!

Lord, I want to thank you for a new day
For allowing me to understand our need to pray
Without Your guidance in hard times
We would all be defeated by the enemy's crime
While we think that we are all alone in this world
It is by our divine connection that we are your treasured pearls
Each step we take is for your glory to perform your deeds
Yet we fall short because we allow Satan to succeed
While we search the skies for a sign from above
You Lord remind us that all our sins have been forgiven
When we begin to acknowledge the truth of these words
The clouds clear and reveal the possibilities in our new day
Each day we give thanks and pray, another path is revealed
Yet wander through life hoping to one day close "the deal"
Each day we wake up with the hope to feel the sun on our face
And should look forward to walk in the light
that is allowed by God's grace
So when you close your eyes just remember what you need to say
Thank you Lord for giving us all a new day!

A Lonely Night

While I sit up at night looking into space
My tears were so large as they rolled down my face
Another lonely night had been spent without love
The question I asked to the one who sits above
"They say there is someone for everyone on earth
So why have I only met the ones who don't value my worth?"
One by one the people I have met were the ones I sent away
Because instead of being for real, they only wanted to play
Each line that I've heard was just one more to refuse
So I wait for the right person to appear before I choose
After a while you get tired of going through the bull
Each time I give love a try it's my heart that gets pulled
Now don't get me wrong because real love would be so worth it
The question that I have is, "when will my heart meet its true fit?'
When can I meet someone who has something for me
The person who is for real and wants to turn I to we
When will I find someone who has a plan of their own
The person who can laugh and cry but refuses to be left alone
When will I find someone who my heart says that you are right
This way I can turn away from another lonely night!

A Pain From The Past

Hello my friends, my family, or anyone who will listen
You don't have to be saved, you may not even be a Christian
But this message I have today is one you have tried to avoid
The angels of Heaven have spoken while Spirit fills your void
Now we all have something that we are afraid to reveal
We have moved on from the past that we felt had to be sealed
What happened to us that caused our memory of deep pain
Will one day be revealed by the blessing of the Lord's rain
We are not alone in what has happened as a child
Too many people hold on to the pain that has taken away our smile
Whether it was neglect, rape, or child abuse
We are not to blame for those moments for which there was no excuse
We have carried the memories that have impacted our story
We need to forgive the moments of our past and focus on God's glory
To forget these times that may never be
So all we can do is forgive the person or people of that misery
Face the time that has destroyed our hidden smile
Because until we forgive, every step may seem like a mile
So today we ask the Lord to allow us to move forward
We pray He takes away our pain from the past

He Felt The Lord's Touch

Today we had a visitor from another house
While he was welcomed by all, it became quiet as a mouse
The preacher was a black man who came to share
The message he would give made you squirm in your chair
He opened up with some photos of what he had been through
As the slide show began, he showed what all need to do
The preacher revealed that the Lord asked him a question
"Can you adjust to the new surroundings' this was a suggestion
The Lord told him that his new people would be white
Uncomfortable at first, but he understood the Lord was right
As the members came, he began to accept and welcomed them in
Each person who entered the service did so with a grin
They all found a new home in the house of the Lord
One by one they came as the preacher could only applaud
Until one of the members who was a white male revealed
My father questioned, "Why do I come to
this place, tell me what you feel"
His father asked his son, "Why do you worship here?"
So he visited The House and the vision became so clear
The father who's white and didn't understand, got baptized today
Hugging the black preacher and felt the Holy Spirit on this special day
The vision the Lord revealed became his blessing to all
As the members grew in volumes that came from God's call
This man of the cloth revealed where he didn't have that much
As he stood, applauded the preacher who felt the Lord's touch

You Will All Be Tested

On a cloudy day a voice came out so clear
Humble yourself so that it's my voice that you hear
For I am your God, the one known as The Almighty
While all call out in pain and misery
Too many people forget who I Am every day
It's not until they have a problem, do they decide to pray
You know who you are, you all know who I mean
Each day you awaken, you only consider me a dream
The time has come for me to show the world who I Am
I will no longer be fooled by those who only know me in a jam
Those who call out without knowing my true heart
Each person who cries out without doing their part
"Lord, help me, forgive me for my foolish ways
Allow me another chance to correct my mistaken days
Lord allow me to straighten out the time you've invested
That is when I heard the Lord say, "You will all be tested"

I Gave You

Today the Lord sent a text to all who have a phone
The call came up restricted so you left the Lord alone
Each time He called out you pushed the word decline
This saddened the Lord because His love was pushed behind
I gave you life and you accepted it each day
When I called out you pushed me away
I gave you health and you accepted it each day
When I came to say hello, you told me to go away
I gave you food so you wouldn't be hungry
Yet when I came you said, "Please get away from me"
I gave you something to drink so you wouldn't be thirsty
Yet when I came, you said, "Please let me be"
I gave you all you needed so that you would be okay
Yet when I came to hear your voice you told me to go away
So when you needed me and I didn't come to you
Just remember the words you said and what you told me to do
So when you call out to me because you are in pain
Just remember your words as my tears flowed like rain
All I ever asked was for you to love me back
You couldn't understand me because your spirit was in lack
All I ever wanted was to show you what you needed to do
Hopefully one day your heart will open and
your eyes will see what I gave you

What You Didn't Do!

Attention everyone who feels they know it all
Please pull up a chair and sit down for my final call
While you have had the luxury of living every single day
Why my children is it so hard for you to simply pray
Each and every one of you that come to my House has your own reason
Some come to give thanks for the week, others come for a season
While you live in the here and now only for your own greed
Don't you get tired when someone only knows you for their own need
You treat others with very little respect each and every day
How can you call yourself a Christian when you refuse to pray?
While you live in a world of hope and sacrifice
Do you really think you are in a position to roll the dice?
How do you know you will wake up to see another day?
You forget my name and you continue to forget to pray
Why do so many call out for a loved one to me?
How do you feel you have the right when darkness comes from Thee?
Has it ever occurred to you that I allow you to fall?
I want your attention and to get you to make that call
Yet you continue to live life like you are the Chosen One
So when I bring my pain that is when you decide to run
How would you like me to turn away and abandon you?
Because your day is coming when I will remember what you didn't do!

Hate Won't Win

Hello everybody within the sound of my voice
Listen to my spirit because you won't have a choice
Now everybody here can say whatever you'd like
When I'm through, they will be asked to take a hike
While we all sit here and say we are not prejudice
The truth of the matter is that hate resides in most of us
When you dislike someone because of the color of their skin
This is a form of prejudice that is felt from within
When you form a negative opinion of someone you don't know
Then the question is asked, "How far will your hate go?"
When you have formed an opinion of someone by their religion
Then you have a prejudice inside that shows where you haven't been
How long will you allow the devil to live within you
What will it take before you realize what you must do
While crime and murder headline the news everyday
What will it take before each of us turns hate away
How long must we allow senseless killing to rule the world?
War in other countries is the sign of destruction to every boy and girl
Crime and hate are the roots that show where we have been
Hope we can one day realize that hate won't win

A Daughter Will Always Want Her Daddy

Today I shed a tear for my own son
While I was proud of his accomplishments,
I was sad about what he'd done
Now don't get me wrong we are human and all make mistakes
Yet I wonder how long he will remain blind
and if he realizes what's at stake
My son has two beautiful daughters by two different ladies
While he shows them both his love I can only wonder how this can be.
The older daughter was his heart, yet because
of her mother he turned away
Now this isn't the reason that I feel the pain his girl has today
While his daughter loves her daddy and she calls out when she can
Only to be turned away because her father has a different plan
Now the second girlfriend is very selfish and pulls him away
Only wanting her child to be loved without
the first child given the time of day
Slowly the older child feels neglected and soon begins to express her pain
While she may never speak of her hurt as her tears flow like rain
Now my son doesn't understand that this pain will run deep
He must address his older daughter's pain if
he wants her attention to keep
While I have addressed the situation with my son he said okay
I can only hope he thinks about what I have to say
Son! Remember, you are the one that both girls will have in their heart
Just remember her hurt is something you can stop if you do your part

Who Are You?

Last night while all may have been quiet I had
a dream and you were not part of it
While I laid there with tears in my eyes
I seemed blinded because you kept telling me your lies
When we met you told me all you thought I wanted to hear
As time passed by all I found was your hidden fear
Who are you because I seem to have hit a wall
Searching for the love who never made the right call
Who are you and what have you done with my sight
When I called your name the only response was not tonight
Who are you because I never seem to hear you call my name
Each time I reached out for you, all I got was someone else's blame
Who are you really trying to be when I'm not around
When will you realize I'm a person with
feelings and not someone's clown
This is not a game, so please don't underestimate me
if you're not the one then just please let me be
Take your time because I know what it takes to be true
My love, my devotion and my respect all ask the question "who are you?"

Let Me

Today I woke up with tears on my face
Thinking about the moment you allowed me in your space
Each time I think of the moment I met you
It takes me to a place I don't know what to do
Let me be the one who takes away your fears
Come and let me be the one who wipes away the tears
Each day that I rise up from the bed where I lay
Let me be the one who remembers the love in your eyes
As the time passes by, I think back to where we've been
Let me take away the pain and replace it with a grin
Sunshine comes to the skies to brighten up each day
Let me be the one who can show you a special way
While we are living good or even living bad
Take a moment to allow your heart to feel how to be free
While we take a trip, all I ask is that you let me

Don't Complain

Hello to everyone who needs someone to hear
While you go through somethings that may bring you a tear
Don't worry about the problems that may come your way
You have been gifted by the Lord to receive a new season today
When you realize a problem is part of your new education
Then you will realize that his lessons are part of your frustrations
He doesn't bring you bumps for any reason at all
The path you are placed on might come without any warning or call
Yet when you trust, he is with you and knows what you need
Through the will of his hands is the blessings he will feed
Don't worry how long things look because you may never understand
Just know and trust his word because we are all a part of his plan
Today you are awakened for his own plan and purpose
When you realize he is in control of the spirt in all of us
Thank the Lord because you are not worthy of what he has already given
Can you honestly say if it wasn't for GOD'S
grace that you would still be living
Take a moment, take a knee, and raise your hands to the sky
Because once you really think about your
life, you will never question why
The Lord brought the sun out, the Lord gave you his grace
While others go through struggles, yet he still shines on your face
So the next time you call out and feel it's always in vain
Take a look at the person next to you who doesn't
have your blessings before you complain

How Many Times Did You?

The preacher asked a question to everyone today
You got up this morning to hear what the Lord had to say
Take a moment to think about your own yesterday
Did you take out any moment to be grateful and pray
You go through your life expecting to receive everything
Why do you really feel like you are entitled to anything
Each step you take may one day be your last
How often have you said that time goes by so fast
Each day that you are awakened is another day by Thee
How many times has the Lord came to hear you
Why do you continue to ignore what you need to do
Each step that you take as the Lord guides your way
Will bring you closer to the kingdom of his today
Yesterday was a blessing as he guided you through
Don't ever think you could've made it without his hands on you
Each vision of tomorrow will show you his might
As yesterday passed he made sure you were alright
We complain, we cry out, we get angry at what we do
The question of today is how many times did you?

Mommy How I Miss You

Now everybody has somebody that they care about
Even the lonely people who want to scream or shout
Yet when you think about all you've been through
Today I found out how much I miss you
It's easy to miss somebody when your thoughts are of another
But what do you do when that person is your mother
Not every parent cares or is there in your time of need
Yet a real mother is special because she knows when your heart bleeds
Even when you feel that she may not always be your friend
Trust her above any other person even when you're at the end
Not every mother may reveal herself or her bleeding heart
But trust and believe without her, you wouldn't have gotten a start
Not every mother has been there when you needed her hand
Do you realize that this doesn't mean she didn't understand
Think back to the times when you would reach out to her
Did you see her smile or frown when her tears made you a blur
As you grew older, did you begin to understand why
Mom wanted you to be the best but all she could do was cry
Now you're all grown up and you know what you must do
Thank your mother, an tell her how I Miss YOU

You Have Issues

Now let's talk about something that most people fear
Please pull up a seat or maybe you should leave here
Everybody comes from a past that had its own impact
So before we begin you must acknowledge this fact
Your childhood may have been one you chose to forget
Some may have enjoyed the memory while others regret
The parents that you have may have left an impression
While others cause so much pain that it shows in your expression
Yet instead of facing your past or getting over the pain
How many feel as if you have been left out in the rain
Before you judge someone you need to really view yourself
Know who you are so you find out your own true wealth
The pain or happy moments have brought you to this point
How often did you tell your parents you wanted to leave their joint
While your childhood may have created who you are to this day
Do you face your past or do you still live in disarray
Because you haven't got over your anger or the hate
Then all you have become is a person who has sealed their fate
To heal from a childhood that wasn't your fault at all
It will take a strong spirt that will answer the rescue call
This won't be easy but this is something you need to do
Let's take the first step by admitting that we all have issues

I'm Proud Of You

Today I watched a television show called "The Voice"
So many people came to apply, yet so few were given a choice
There was a thirteen year old girl who began
to sing melodically like a bird
All the judges turned their chairs for a look at
the person whose voice they heard
While the girl sang her song, she did so without any fears
Each person listened closely and intently as their eyes released their tears
Her parents stood by just as proud as they could be
She continued to sing her song so loud and effortlessly
The camera angle switched back stage to catch a glimpse of her dad
As he wiped away his tears it was his spirit that made him glad
The Lord stepped in to guide his little girl at age thirteen
As the world got a glimpse of the beauty that had never been seen
She finished her song and all the judges stood up to applaud
This little angel had proven to the world that she was gifted by the Lord
While tears flowed in the house and everyone
gave her nothing but praise
The judges had to admit that they were simply blown away
At such a very young age she was so poised and so confident
The judges all asked for a chance to work with her God-given talent
Her father came over and wrapped his arms
around his tiny but precious girl
As everyone clapped, her parents began to
feel the love from the whole world
The judges came to ask her what will you do now
The little girl looked to the sky as she responded with a big WOW
Her father came over and hugged her and said it's up to you what you do
With tears on his face he whispered I'm so proud of you

Why Are We?

Now everyone should think about the question why
And ask did you come into my life as a partner or as a lie
When we first met did you just see a pretty face
Or was I just somebody that you needed to use or wanted to replace
Why are you here occupying space in my heart
Are you here to help my journey or just playing a part
When we first met, you promised me the world
Can you still make me smile or was I just a temporary thrill
Ladies, I have a question addressed to you
When your man has a desire that needs attention, what will you do
Every couple has problems that will arise without warning
My question, "Is there a real solution or will
it have to wait until morning?"
Once we commit to one another will that really be it
When temptation presents itself, will you hold strong or decide to submit
There are always paths, choices and people that can tear you apart
The question remains, will you be part of my future instead of my past
As we walk down this road seeking the answers to life
Have you become the woman of my yesterday or my future wife
Beauty comes in different ways and is in the eyes of the beholder
Has your heart fallen for mines or has it been lured by another
Let's be real because time isn't promised to anyone
Are we here to commit or to just have fun
Let's explore our desires and check the games at the door
While we ponder a future together and hope for so much more
So before we consider the best path for you and me
Let's take a step back and ask the question, Why Are We?

Not Me

A powerful word came to the church on this bright sunny day
While all the people gathered to hear what the preacher had to say
The message was so strong that I had to stay in my place
When I listened to the Word it brought tears to my face
Church folks come to service each Sunday for a whole lot of reasons
How many serve the Lord for the Lord in every single season
While people come to church and claim to be true Christians
How many clear their thoughts for the Lord so they can really listen
You claim to know the Lord yet you fail to observe Thee
Each time He delivered your request you
turned your back and said "not me"
The blessing the Lord promised came from His own chosen direction
Yet your eyes were only looking for your own windows of perfection
How often were you called upon to walk the path of Thee
Yet you didn't recognize the Lord's call, so your response was "not me"
Church folk walk around quoting the Bible
and claim their way is always right
Yet when the Lord calls on them, all they can
say is "sorry stranger not tonight"
When they meet a soul that's out of the circle that they know
They fail to acknowledge that the Lord's hand
was showing them where to go
Pay attention to the words of a person who
may appear to be a total stranger
They could be the Lord's messenger sent to
keep you from hidden danger
The day will come when the Lord will return to show the face of Thee
When He asks "did you call?" Hopefully
your answer won't be "NOT ME"

When You Lose It All

Well you have finally hit rock bottom my friend
You had so much before the Lord showed you the end
While you had been given so much it never seemed to be enough
So now you have to start all over and believe me that will be tough
When you had the world at your beckon call
Did you ever think the day would come for you to lose it all?
How many times were you given another
chance to help another or even share?
Yet you ignored the warning signs because you really didn't care
How many people did you turn away because you felt like a king
You forgot where you came from without earning anything
The Lord decided to step in and humble you tonight
The time had to remind you who you really
are because you weren't living right
You need to remember who you are and who you need to be
While you struggle through hard times, you still belong to Thee
You must crawl before you walk; walk before you run
I gave you everything; I gave the world my only son
Know your place, remember who I am when I call
Remember how life is or you will remember when you too will lose it all

The Loss Of A Loved One

Hello everyone who has come to pay their respects
Please take a seat even though you may feel like a wreck
Today is a celebration and yet you feel so hurt
While we sit and cry on the inside, our hearts have been put on alert
You never realize how much value someone has while in your path
Until they are taken away and you begin to do the math
We gather at these sad times and ask the question why
The answer will never be enough as we look towards the sky
Many tears will fall today and the pain will run very deep
Yet today is a day of memories that we all are here to keep
So let the tears fall today and you may even let out a scream
Only you know what your pain is all about or so it seems
While the loved one lived they may have been a royal pain
Yet when times became too difficult only they understood your rain
The loved one may have sometimes plucked your nerves
Yet only their love was allowed to step inside your painful curves
The loved one seemed to listen to you while you would always complain
Yet they understood you in your happy times and your pain
So today you are here to say goodbye and believe me this won't be fun
Just take a moment to grieve the loss of the
one you call your LOVED One

The Devil Asked For You

Did you wake up this morning with trouble on your mind
Why did you think that I would be so hard to find
Trouble is my name and I will tell all who ask
Don't ever forget who I am or your spirit simply won't last
The devil is what many people call me
While most curse my name, happiness would be an impossibility
Whenever you're in trouble and you call on your mighty GOD
Did you ever think to ask who sent you that lighting rod
When you lost all hope and felt your back against the wall
Who do you really think would come to answer your foolish call
The Devil is my name and I can grant you all your wishes
Just like food for thought, I provide your food on my dishes
While the Lord causes you pain to educate your soul
The devil just gives you what you want so you will do as you are told
Enjoy my gifts and keep in mind they all come with a price
Just know that one day I will come to collect your soul for sacrifice
So please call on me for your needs as I tell you what to do
When you answer my call, just remember the Devil asked for you

She Said "I Love You Daddy"

So many fathers in this world are loved by their children
Yet they never hear a word because a legal paper isn't filed
So many fathers have to experience this pain inside
Because the mother of their children has her own foolish pride
The mother has her own hidden agenda
She uses the children as a tool to get a court defender
A lot of hurt is caused by the system leaving
fathers without their children
That's when the father hears the words, "Daddy where have you been?"
There are so many fathers who don't even know they have children
Because the mother has hidden this fact until her court papers are filed
Too many ladies think outside the norm and just interested in the cash
They use their children as leverage so they can obtain money very fast
The pain caused, hurt and lasting effects, is
not a concern or is thought about
Until one day the child grows up and the
truth causes them to say, "Wow"
Years go by without knowing their real daddy
Yet the child will always question mom about their whereabouts
Until the child turns to their mother and says I am done
So many years you have hidden the truth about my only daddy
Why have you told me lies about where my father could be?
That was the moment I found my child and
they said, "I love you Daddy"

Today Is A Good Day

I woke up this morning and felt the sun on my face
It doesn't matter where I am, just know I am in a good place
I rose up from my bed and felt my feet hit the floor
Thank you Jesus for this blessing and yes I am hoping for more
I went to wash my face and get something to eat
Each blessing given was felt and I was filled with gratefulness
I know somebody somewhere didn't have any of these things
So no matter what else happens today it's my destiny the Lord brings
Each person I meet today is a face I won't soon forget
Many will say hello while others can bring me regret
We go through the day hoping to complete our plans
The funny thing is only God allows us to stand
We go on with our day hoping we make it through
But did we ever say thank you Lord as He watched over us?
Do you ever take the time to acknowledge He is our King?
Or are you someone who feels you are entitled to everything?
Understand your purpose is to serve the Lord in every way
Once you realize this, you can say, "Today was a good day"

Hello Tomorrow!

Today I had to sit down and think about our sorrow
While my eyes grew with tears, I could only say hello tomorrow
We are not promised that tomorrow will ever come
Yet we must be thankful for another day and
remember where we've come from
Time may pass without leaving its mark on our day
If we don't learn from our mistakes then we've wasted another day
We hope for a bright future as we learn from the past
Tomorrow is always waiting yet we wish for it too fast
Know that each day has a meaning of its own
You are the reason for someone's today and you are never all alone
Take stock of yesterday and enjoy what the day brings
No one promised tomorrow yet its hope that we sing
Each day is a present and we receive it in our own way
Are you sure you are grateful for the blessing you got today?
Think back to yesterday and what today brought
Have you learned from your past or are you still in court?
No matter what you've been through, even sorrow has a price
Be grateful you are still here so you can roll the dice
Stand up to everyone and learn in today's sorrow
This will be the moment when you can say hello tomorrow!

I Remember You

Have you ever taken the time to remember what you have done?
Think back to your past when you felt life was fun
Have you ever wondered how you made it this far?
Remember those moments when your life was a war
Each time you felt alone with nowhere to turn
Only then were you willing to finally listen and learn
Instead of calling yourself fortunate or even lucky
Did you ever consider the fact that you were blessed by Thee?
How often did you receive a blessing that you didn't deserve?
While you were rescued from your situation because you had the nerve
The nerve or the courage, both made you finally stand
Only then did you realize how much you can
Instead of looking forward for luck or depending on hope
Only to be disappointed when your best friend says "Nope"
Yet the Lord never failed you in your time of need
When you realize it's by the Lord's grace the devil heeds
So think about those times while you think about what to do
Those will be the moments you tell the Lord I remember you

Daddy Please

While every child grows up trying to please their dad
There are so many children seeking the father they never had
When their mothers tell the children of how dad was a story
That's the times they remember as their mother's only glory
While every child doesn't have a story to remember
Some fathers left home before the beginning of September
Daddy please come home and show me the right way
Yet the cries in the night are never heard in the day
Daddy please come back, I'm so sorry for whatever I did
As the tears flow from the eyes of every abandoned kid
Daddy, please give me a chance to make everything alright
Yet little did the child know that it was never their fight
While every child grows older with the loss of another
Daddy please is the phrase that their tears cry to their mother
When you look into a child's eyes and they look back to you
Think and remember their pain before you do what you do
While you may not remember the moment you made your child cry
Think about the future and try to stay for a while
The next time you decide to have a moment, I suggest you freeze
Because you don't want your child to say, "Daddy please"

Couldn't Sleep Last Night

When people lay down to finally rest
Do they really know whether or not they will awaken?
Will they ever pass God's test
We complete our tasks each day and wonder if it was the Lord's agenda
Do you ever go over the details as you try to remember
You close your eyes trusting that you will awaken each morning after
You trust in the Lord, while others feel they are forsaken
Why do some people have a restless night tossing and turning
Do you remember each day's lesson
If so, do you put them into practice
As we each live and breathe mistakes are inevitable
Do we reflect on our mishaps, missteps and
our actions and bother to pray
How many times has the Lord given you everything including grace
So why do you continue to fail Him when
all He asks you is for first place
Allow the Lord to work himself into your heart so he can use you
How long will you fight His will, how long
will you run and refuse to serve Him
You wonder why the Lord comes to you in the middle of the night
That's because you don't listen when He
calls before you are ready to fight
You toss, turn, you struggle and tell yourself it will be alright
Then you wonder why you couldn't sleep last night!

Let's Make Things Right

Today I watched a television show that brought me to tears
It was about a doctor who wanted to make a difference and erase all fear
He was new to this hospital and he arrived late one night
No one knew his intentions as he yelled, "Let's make things right!"
Too many policies and too many old rules
The time has come for us to fire all the fools
No more policies that restrict us from saving lives
When faced with a problem we will do all we can and never give up
The first call will be to all those who don't believe
They will be fired because it is our patients we care about
They deserve all of your attention and are to be your first concern
This will be the new policy that will be put into place
So if you can't abide by this, please rest assured
You will be fired first and I will be the one showing you the door
There is a new way to operate and we will do all we can
No matter how rich or poor
No matter if you are a woman or man
This hospital is here to help everyone who is in need
No longer will policy stop you from being doctors and I hope you agree
Today is a new day and if you don't agree with me tonight
Tell me any problems, let's make things right!

A New Day

Lord, I want to thank you for a new day
For allowing me to understand our need to pray
Without Your guidance in hard times
We would all be defeated by the enemy's crime
While we think that we are all alone in this world
It is by our divine connection that we are your treasured pearls
Each step we take is for your glory to perform your deeds
Yet we fall short because we allow Satan to succeed
While we search the skies for a sign from above
You Lord remind us that all of our sins have been forgiven
When we begin to acknowledge the truth of these words
The clouds clear and reveal the possibilities in our new day
Each day we give thanks and pray another path is revealed
Yet wander through life hoping to one day close "the deal"
Each day we wake up with the hope to feel the sun on our face
And should look forward to walk in the light
that is allowed by God's grace
So when you close your eyes just remember what you need to say
Thank you, Lord, for giving us all a new day!

Sit Down And Listen

Today I met two strangers that was very hard to receive
While I walked through a dining area noticing a man named Steve
The voice of the Lord reached out and told me to sit down
So I approached his table and asked" May I please sit down with you?"
Steve and his wife smiled and said yes if that's what you need to do
They both spoke of the Lord and revealed their own glorious story
While I listened to their voices, they both spoke of God's glory
Steve spoke of how he was once so much like me
He also found the Lord and turned his life around just to follow Thee
We spoke about the Lord for a while and his spirit sounded so sincere
Now I was the type of person who really didn't care
Yet this couple was special and got my undivided attention
While I began to explain my concerns with some, I failed to mention
They pointed out to me that the Lord needed me to grow
They showed me the direction that they felt I needed to know
Read the Word, the Lord has been waiting on your actions
Nothing will change until you give the Lord
your life without any distraction
Read the Word, that will add to your very own testimony
Once you understand your purpose, that's
when you will become God's glory
Read his Word, that's when you become a true Christian
The first thing you will need to do is for you to sit down and listen

The Monster From Within

While so many people go through a hurt or hidden pain
They hold this feeling inside until their eyes show the rain
As we endure the hurt from someone who has control
We take on their abuse until our own story begins to unfold
Now think back to when it started and the pain grew through the years
While we never understand the abuse that shows in our tears
These times that we felt someone turn to drugs or alcohol
These were the hurtful moments that we couldn't understand at all
Yet being a child, we could only feel the pain shown to us
While we sat by to watch our loved one lose all of their trust
As we grew up and watched the situations only get worse
Some parents grew angry while others would just curse
As a child we have to stand by and absorb all the abuse we witness
Until we grow up to learn that we don't have to accept any of this
Your mommy or daddy or even a school teacher
The abuser could be anyone; it could even by a preacher
Yet we carry this pain and act out in total discuss
These are the results when no one cared to
question what's really troubling us
While some may never be able to face the
one who caused them their pain
Yet the anger and hate inside may one day
cause you to show others insane
Please try to forgive someone so your own healing can begin
The day has arrived for you to face the monster from within

We Need To Cry

Well please sit down so that I can explain to you why
Instead of holding back everything inside, your spirit needs to cry
Think about what's hurting you inside and let it out
Instead of holding it inside of your heart, let's try to give it a shout
Everybody has something that has made their spirit feel so very sad
Yet until we acknowledge the pain inside, how
can you move past what we had
Life is full of lessons that not everyone will be able to understand
The bumps in our past will allow us to become
a stronger woman or a man
So matter what your pain is, and trust me it's not going to be fun
How long will you hide the hurt that has your heart on the run
Stand up and face your fears and don't let them hide
Tell fear he isn't welcomed anymore and kick him to the side
When a man shows his tears, he is showing his very own pain
This is a mature man who reveals his heart in God's rain
Let your pain out, it's time to set your past free
How long do you want to carry the cross that was nailed to THEE
When you begin to heal and let the pain of the past go
Each time your hurt tries to return just simply say no
Rise up from your past as you begin heal, as the Lord shows you why
Allow your eyes to water because your heart needs to cry

That's My Child

Today I had a dream about the one I call my dad
Not understanding the reason but my heart grew very sad
Since the last time we spoke had been so long ago
The face that was revealed told me he had to go
My father was a man who did the best he could
While some might argue this fact, I know I never would
Until you know the whole story of where someone has been
You should never judge them because that's not something you can win
When I lay down to sleep and on this night I didn't pray
The Lord brought my father's face to me on his last day
The vision that I had was of him smiling as a child
As his picture appeared in my dreams, I could only try to smile
While we had our differences, I learned that he meant me well
Even as I grew older thinking why did he put me through his own hell
While I grew older, that's when I would begin to understand
He was my father, and he was grooming me to become a better man
As children we may never understand the intentions of a DAD
Yet as an adult and when you have kids, that's when you will understand
Not everyone have the blessing of their father in their life to look out
So for those who do have their pops in their life,
hopefully you appreciate what I'm talking about
My father may not have been a perfect dad
but he gave me the chance to smile
So I thank you Dad for your lesson as he
smiled back and said that's my child

Where I've Been

Now pull up a chair because you need to sit down
While I reveal my soul, you should understand I'm not fooling around
Now each of us has a past moment that gave us a tear
As we grow older and wiser while others will live in fear
While we try to cover the hurt or our past pain
Life has a way of leaving its own heartbreak, while some call it a stain
Some may find that the hurt was a lesson or a good thing
While others try to escape or erase the pain it could bring
Everything you face in life will leave its own paper trail
Whether we realize it or not, without the Lord we are destined to fail
While we fail at somethings in life they may
only be a temporary set back
That should be the crossroad in your journey
that will determine where you're at
Each person who calls out for you in some way to receive a helping hand
May have their own reasons that you won't ever begin to understand
Just know that each struggle is not meant for lose or win
Hopefully you will learn from this moment that
has shown the world where you've been
Don't judge me and I won't be a judge of you
Let's just grow together as one and let the Lord show us what to do
Today is the day that we will rise up and learn how to win
Because we have become trustworthy, obedient, and
loving; which will reveal where we have been

Are You Ready To Confess?

Now let's look at the mirror so you can really see you
That's the reflection which is revealed to those without a clue
When you really take this moment, does it ever make you say wow!
If you do, then maybe you're the one who acts
like they are holier than THOU
Now don't get me wrong because everyone should feel great
So let's take some time to reflect and set the record straight
You're no better than anyone else, and yet you act like you are
Think about your actions when you're around
others when they've gone too far
When your coworkers, family and friends
go out and you never get invited
Maybe you're the problem and that may be why you feel slighted
Do you ever brag about what you have without considering other's ideas
Maybe because everyone else in your circle can't
get past your attitude of I don't care
Do you ever take a look around and find yourself all alone
Maybe it's because the time has come for
you to put down your cell phone
When you go to church, is it for the Word or a fashion show
That's when the real question becomes clear, why you really go
Can you name three friends that just enjoy you for your company
Take a long hard look around and you might
ask the question how this can be
Now that you have asked these questions,
hopefully you can pass this test
Otherwise you will need to go back to the mirror and start to confess

I Feel You

Take a moment from your busy day
Let's think about everything in your life that became your today
Take a another moment to think of where you would be
When you remember your past, I hope you gave thanks to Thee
So many times you were lifted up from all hell
Did you ever think that your life could turn out so well
How often did you ponder on what you might have to do
This is the time when you acknowledge the Lord by saying I feel you
Each day is a challenge that everyone must face
While life might knock you down, it was
GOD who put you back in place
Each time you felt all alone or just didn't know what to do
These were the moments the Lord touched
your spirit and you said I feel you
Each day you were awakened to do the Lord's will
Every time you opened your eyes was a moment
the Lord told the devil to chill
Each day the sun rises is another day we are shown what we must do
Did you ever think the day would come when
you might say Lord I feel you
Remember where you were when your back was against the wall
Think of all the promises by friends, yet they allowed you to fall
Just remember yesterday when you rise up against
everyone that stands in God's way
Know the Lord's got your back as you rise up
and remember your Lord today
When your spirit directs your heart on what it needs for you to do
Close your eyes and feel the Lord's hands touch
your heart and say I FEEL YOU

What's The Plan

I was awakened this morning with tears on my face
Not knowing or understanding the feelings that were placed in my space
While I laid in my bed trying to understand
The question I asked the LORD is GOD what's the plan
Tears on my face that I couldn't begin to know why
Even as I laid still questioning the Holy Spirit why
Until finally I rose from the bed to stand on my feet
Still not understanding the reason or whom I was to meet
Lord thank you for allowing me to see another day
While I have your attention may I know your plan for me today
Each time we wake, it's only by your grace and that I understand
Yet the tears that flow down my face has to be part of your plan
When will the day come that you allow all people to believe
Even as we live another day it's not a moment
that anyone earns what they receive
When will the day come so that we can all live without any fears
Even as we live another day to receive your
blessing that sometimes bring tears
When will the day come when this forsaken world can unite
Even as we live for you, our hearts know that this world isn't rite
When will the day come that all the hate will go away
Then the clouds came with a voice that told me this won't happen today
Too long this world has chosen to only listen and follow man
So how can you ever ask me to tell the world
of non-believers what's the plan

Are You Ready For The Rain?

Do you know someone who has a lot of pain inside
While they show the world a smile it's their pain they can't hide
Do you know someone who always shows the world attitude
While you show them respect, they seem to only come off being rude
Yet when you ask them what is really going on
Their answer is the same, "don't ask me what wrong"
The time will come when they will reach out for you
That will be the moment when you must decide what you're going to do
Not everyone knows how to confide or trust
Yet don't you take this personal because it will cause them to fuss
Nobody knows how to reveal the pain they really feel
Just know this pain is so deep it becomes hard to reveal
The person or the family might not ever begin to understand
So the person you want to know may not
know how to tell you their plan
Just be ready for the day when they become ready to talk
The time will come as a surprise when they say let's take a walk
Just know your time will be precious and don't say a word
Be ready to hear their pain as you will be shocked at what you heard
This walk will be long because it may take you back some years
As they reveal their pain that's been carried through their tears
When people are ready to share all of their deepest pain
The real question will be are you ready for their rain?